HOW TO DRESS YOUR BEST

HOW TO DRESS YOUR BEST

Ellie-Jean Royden

Discover Your Style and Curate
a Wardrobe That Actually Works

Contents

Int

roduction

Just wear what you love: it's such a simple, enticing message. One day women said 'no more' to the strict rulebook we felt we had to follow, and mentally threw it into the fire. You know the one; it said you have to wear black to look more slim, never wear stripes that make you look wide, never dare to stand out or take up space. It was a rulebook based on avoiding things you might love because there was apparently always something fundamentally wrong with you. It was a period where any descriptor applied to a woman became something she had to fix. Too tall? Look shorter. Too short? Look taller. Too skinny? Look more curvy. Too fat? Look more svelte. The perfect body truly didn't exist and, if it was out there, you certainly didn't have it – that much was clear. Eventually, somewhere down the line, we got sick of thinking so hard about what clothes to put on our bodies and collectively agreed on a new law: just buy the things you like.

But now I see a new problem. You are standing in front of your wardrobe, breathing heavy, lip trembling, gazing at the rails of clothing in front of you. You refuse to look at the dresses, handbags and old shoes on the floor that you yanked off the hangers and flung across the room in frustration. Those clichéd words settle on the tip of your tongue: 'I have nothing to wear'. In a world where we can find new things we like every day, with some websites adding hundreds of new clothes weekly, and an infinite number of outfits appearing on our social media feeds that we can purchase with a click of a button, the 'just buy what you like' principle is failing. New trends, rebranded as 'aesthetics' (such as dark academia, cottage-core, coquette – see more in the glossary on page 220), appear constantly, offering a simple archetype you could easily slip into – until the next one comes along. Our wardrobes have become a mishmash of styles that make no coherent sense, ensuring the process of putting a decent outfit together on a daily basis is nothing short of a battle.

The reality is, what we like on the hanger or on Instagram isn't always what we like to see on our bodies or in our closets. Those cute slingback heels might feel like a treat, until you remember you live on a farm, and you walk out of your door into a muddy field every morning, and so they sit growing dust in your wardrobe forever. Or, perhaps, you are in love with chunky Dr Marten boots but when you put them on all you experience is pain, sweaty feet and blisters because you live in sunny southern Spain. What you are attracted to is not always what works best for you.

Perhaps you sit on the other side of the spectrum and you don't know what you love. The idea of following what makes you feel good sounds amazing, but if you're not sure what does make you feel this way then the mantra becomes difficult to put into action. There is almost no guidance for those of us who feel uninspired by clothing yet want to feel confident and comfortable when getting dressed every day. The new 'just wear what you like' rulebook leaves many of us high and dry, with no guidance for feeling more empowered by clothing.

Struggling to know what to wear myself, I became preoccupied with solving this issue. While I was supposed to be studying French in Canada, I spent my mornings, noons and nights absorbing every piece of information I could dig out of the internet on style theories. Instead of practising French grammar, I studied style systems, colour seasons and body types, and stumbled into a community that believes our bodies are not awkward or problematic, made to be hidden, but unique and exciting canvases that can be intellectually explored, painted on or draped with a myriad fabrics and colours. After these revelations, I became a woman possessed. I had no idea that this obsession would be one others shared and eventually lead to a successful platform, my own business and a new life. While in the midst of my new-found hobby, I was learning just to learn. I felt I finally had the answers to why I looked different, how I could feel truly beautiful for the first time and be a part of a community of women that cared about fashion in the same way I did. I flew to Montreal with my knowledge of *bonjours* and *mercis*

much weaker than it should have been, but with my head packed with information like the significance limb length has on an outfit.

It was in Canada, during my daily trip to the thrift store (which I still miss) that I decided to share my new love of personal style. I made videos on Kibbe body types (page 167) and instantly captured the interest of hundreds of people. One evening I made the video that would change my life. I wore one outfit that did not work for my body and one that did and revealed my body type as the transformational factor. I watched the video hit 10,000 views almost instantly, and by the next morning it had over one million views and I had over 100,000 followers. My email was flooded with people asking me if I could help them find their body type, and so I began Body & Style. I set up my website and, just like that, I had a business. My hobby turned into a passion for helping women find confidence in their bodies and, since then, I have helped nearly 2,000 women find their personal style using my style theories and guided millions of people through my social media pages.

With this book I want to democratise personal style. As a girl growing up in rural Norfolk in England, most of my outfits consisted of wellington boots and a raincoat for trudging through the fields with my lurchers. I was under the impression that style was for someone else: city girls from *The Devil Wears Prada* who all seemed to have walk-in wardrobes and rows of Jimmy Choos, who stride about the streets of New York and work in glamorous offices. It was my stylish and beautiful mum (my best friend) who showed me that personal style doesn't have to look like high heels, giant tulle skirts and oversized blazers like the magazines would have you believe. Style is a tool to help you feel more confident every day, and it can be applied to your dog walks or day at the office as much as it can the runway.

Even though all the information you need to find your personal style is available online, I still receive the same questions from my clients and followers every day. I realised that, instead of trawling the internet, what everyone needs is a one-stop guide to learn what works for them – and this book is just that.

At first glance, these style theories can seem complex and insurmountable; there is so much information out there from different sources, contradictory opinions, and vague explanations, all of which can make your head hurt. However, in this book I will demystify the complicated process of finding your Style Roots (page 22), Body Matrix (page 102), your Colour Season (page 141), and the silhouettes you should wear, making every detail simple and easy to navigate so that you can find yourself, curate yourself and ultimately express yourself. At the end of it all you will come away with a clear idea of the items that should take pride of place in your wardrobe and finally be able to dress your best.

How to use this book

This book is designed to be followed page by page and step by step. By the end you should feel confident enough to curate your perfect wardrobe. Alongside my explanations and breakdowns of the different style methods, I also provide exercises and guides to help you personalise the process.

Although we want to perfect your style, this book itself does not need to remain polished – highlight sections, write notes in the margins, pen your thoughts as you learn. You cannot simply read; you must take action. Feel free to pause occasionally and venture into your wardrobe as though it is Narnia: create outfits, assess the items you find there and reimagine their potential. I am also going to ask you throughout this book to take photographs. Get a camera, whether it be your phone, a digital camera or a polaroid, and document your learnings. Photography is the best way to get objective about your style.

Your style toolbox

In this book I have done the hard work for you and broken down numerous style lessons, systems and methods. I think of each of these as a tool that you can use to level-up your personal style.

I like to imagine a literal box of spanners, screwdrivers and hammers with labels like 'Colour Seasons' (page 102), 'Body Matrix' (page 141) and 'Style Roots' (page 22) – when you pick one of them up and tap your outfit, it magically takes in the lessons from that particular style method. Of course, in reality it's not quite so simple, but the idea still applies. Sometimes you will be happy with your outfit as it

is without any of these tools being applied to it, in which case you can walk out the door with a smile on your face. However, sometimes utilising one of these tools can help you turn an outfit into something that makes you feel more confident and positive. I'll walk you through each of these tools as the book progresses. Not everyone needs the same tools in their toolbox, which is fine. With my help, you can collect the style tools that feel exciting and useful to you and use them when you feel you need them.

01

Find what YOU *love* to WEAR

Why we need constraints

As I emerged from my teen years, I found myself with a wardrobe full of clothing in clashing styles. Some items were very clearly from the grunge aesthetic, others hyper-feminine, some clean and minimal, some bright and colourful and so on. Without direction, it is easy to buy any item you like the look of, resulting in a wardrobe full of clothes that have no cohesion and are impossible to put together.

Having contrasting influences in your wardrobe is not only permissible but encouraged; however, in most cases, having too many different styles leads to a wardrobe that feels messy. Most of us cannot be 100% 'minimalist' or 'dark academia' and masquerade in this singular aesthetic every day (often this leads to bursts of panic-buying items that make no

sense in your wardrobe but offer a glimpse of fashion freedom), so I am by no means suggesting you force yourself into one box. However, adding a few constraints will strengthen the impact of your style.

How to know
what you
really like

If you look at the pieces you are naturally drawn to – whether that be in your closet, on your Pinterest board or in your wildest dreams – you will find patterns and links. Despite the lack of cohesion, your true preferences will be there somewhere in what you have collected. Perhaps the clothes share a colour palette, similar motifs or silhouettes? Maybe you are drawn to rough fabrics, metallic details or soft pinks? You can use these patterns to gather data, for example: rough fabrics might mean you like a natural look, metallic details could mean you like dark styles and pinks might imply you are drawn to feminine items.

Write a list of the elements you see repeated in your wardrobe:

○ Patterns (such as florals, stripes, chevrons)

○ Colours (such as rose pink, sky blue, off-white)

○ Adornments (such as bows, zips, buttons)

○ Fabrics (such as cotton, linen, chiffon)

○ Type of item (such as dresses, coats, jeans)

These repeated elements say something about your choices, for better or for worse. Hold onto this list as this will help you define your style later.

But Ellie-Jean, if I am already drawn to these things, what is the problem? Why is my wardrobe not cohesive?

Sometimes what you love is not as obvious as it may seem. I, for instance, find myself drawn to the style of Jenny Humphrey: the Gothic, glamorous bad girl from the series *Gossip Girl*. Because of this, one might assume that I like dark, edgy styles when actually, with a deeper look, I've realised that I merely love the flamboyance, the daring and the drama of her outfits. This realisation results in a completely different look when applied to my own style. Often, we let obvious conclusions cloud our judgement, so take the time to interrogate *why* you're drawn to certain styles or trends. If I had followed through on my initial assumption that I like edgy, gothic styles, I might have accidentally filled my wardrobe with black lace in an attempt to recreate what I love about Jenny's outfits ... when what I really love is her unusual layering, dramatic silhouettes and neutral tones. It is this confusion that leads to a wardrobe full of conflicting styles, with hints of the real you diluted by a lot of mess.

Defining *your style*

We are all influenced by some styles (by which I mean specific combinations of colour, silhouette and motifs) more than we are others. This preference is our **style identity**: your unique fashion blueprint, the core underpinning of your outfit choices.

With the rise of social media, the amount of fashion inspiration we consume can be overwhelming. Super-niche aesthetics and styles seem to pop up every other week – often it's hard to keep on top of or understand the terminology. It's important to take on board that most of these aesthetics are too restrictive and are in fact reinvented and rebranded styles that have been around for decades, some even centuries, made to cater to internet audiences. Style genres like 'e-girl', 'punk' and 'emo' or perhaps 'preppy', 'old money' or 'coastal grandmother' (see page 220) are often interchangeable; in the real world you could swap the outfits of these apparently distinct aesthetics and they would happily be worn by the same person. These aesthetics are rooted in similar ideas, motivations and desires.

I have defined the patterns behind these motivations and sorted them into eight categories (page 22) – I call these Style Roots. I discovered through my work that many women feel they lack direction for their style, and that their style fluctuates, so they are left with a wardrobe seemingly full of mess that doesn't help to tell a story. Many of the systems I have researched (read more about them on page 166) mostly orbit the idea that 'if you have these features, you

should wear this aesthetic' or they take a step further and imply that there is some cosmic connection between the way you look and your personality. Helpful as these can be for certain style dilemmas, they don't provide a foundation for discovering and applying what you truly like in fashion, and it is this that creates personal style. Women need a simple system that applies their style desires, their motivations and their taste to the clothes they put on their bodies, which can also be used in tandem with other systems, rather than fighting with them.

The eight Style Roots

The Style Roots system is inspired by nature, for example: light, delicate chiffon is rooted in floral petals and fluffy clouds; black lace gowns are rooted in the night sky and shadows; simple shapes are rooted in the unassuming nature of the Mushroom. It's poetic, perhaps even a little pretentious, but these correlations help to easily pinpoint what shapes and styles you truly love. Although you will likely find yourself drawn to elements of all eight Style Roots, focusing on your top three will help you streamline your style and express what is unique about your tastes. In the pages that follow, try to observe which roots you feel most attracted to and don't worry if you don't resonate with every part of the description; we are looking for the best version of yourself. Once you've got to grips with each Style Root, I will help you select your top three and explain how to tie them together.

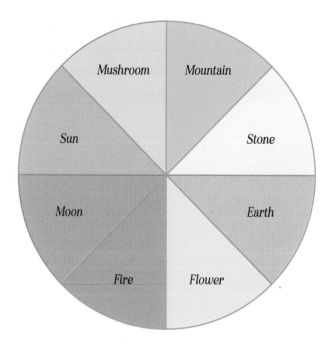

Mushroom

Mountain

Stone

Earth

Flower

Fire

Moon

Sun

ushroom

Mushroom is the minimal, neutral, simple influence in your style. Think of smooth button mushrooms; they are unassuming, neat, symmetrical. You can view the Mushroom Style Root as a clean slate. In nature, the Mushroom root expresses itself as the tide flowing onto the sand, the blades of a grass on dunes and fields of barley melting into the pale blue sky.

When paired with other Style Roots, Mushroom calms the outfit, strips it of complexity and neutralises it. I associate Mushroom with stereotypically classic and 'timeless' styles as it is defined by its lack of elements. The Mushroom root makes an outfit more simple, minimal and clean.

Someone with the Mushroom Style Root is similarly simple in nature. They don't like to look fussy or over the top. They are to the point, authentic and calm. They don't feel the need to draw attention to themself with bells and whistles but, regardless, the simplicity of their style means their personality radiates. They like their space to be uncluttered, only keeping what they need and making sure it is used. When you speak to them, they will have a calm gaze, a soft ease of movement, and will walk with confidence.

Some words associated with the Mushroom Style Root include:

- balanced
- classic
- curated
- clean
- effortless
- elegant
- elevated
- high-quality
- minimal
- modest
- neutral
- put-together
- simple
- sophisticated
- timeless
- understated

Elements in clothing or outfits that make them Mushroom:

Your outfit may have two or more of these elements to make it Mushroom, and certainly not all of them.

Simple colour palette

Mushroom does not try to make a statement with its colours; colours tend to blend. Some ways to achieve this include:

○ **Colour sandwiches:** This is when two items within the same outfit are the same colour. For example, you may have heard the rule that your bag, shoes and belt must match – this is the kind of rule that the Mushroom-rooted would want to follow.

○ **Neutral tones:** Neutrals include shades of brown, grey, beige, white and black – these colours are very simple and unassuming.

○ **Three colours or fewer:** The more colours there are in an outfit, the more of a statement you may make. The less colour you use, the simpler you appear.

○ **Low contrast:** This means the colours you pick for an outfit are not on opposite sides of the spectrum and are close in tone.

Modesty

○ **Moderate lengths:** Extreme shapes, like maxi or mini skirts, contrast with the simplicity of Mushroom.

○ **Limited skin:** There is nothing wrong with showing a little skin, but the Mushroom Style Root won't drive that in an outfit.

Balance

○ From the Mushroom perspective, if an outfit is feeling formal, a little 'undone' influence is needed to counteract this (I mean this in the literal sense – like undoing some buttons) and vice versa. Mushroom prevents an outfit feeling definably formal or relaxed – it should feel in the middle.

- **Sandwiches:** We have already covered colour sandwiches, but this applies to other parts of an outfit too, including shape, size and pattern. For example, when there are two structured elements of an outfit, a third looser or relaxed item will add a harmonious balance to the outfit.

Minimal detail

- Mushroom is motivated by the idea of pulling back, rather than expanding. Therefore, plain fabrics and shapes are more Mushroom than patterned or print fabrics. Similarly, 3D – details like ruffles, pockets, zips or layered textures – would be limited or non-existent in a Mushroom outfit.

Simple or minimal layers

- Too many layers will add detail to an outfit, whereas Mushroom strips an outfit back to a simpler form.

Clean silhouettes

- Frayed edges, un-ironed fabrics and rough fabrics make an outfit 'messier', which to someone with a Mushroom Style Root is undesirable.

- Clean lines include neat edges, uninterrupted silhouettes and straight lines.

Timeless silhouettes

- Breton jumper
- Cigarette pants
- Straight jeans
- Silk midi skirt
- Fitted button-down
- White t-shirt
- White trainers
- Ballet flats
- Silver pendant necklace

Mountain

M ountain is the formal, professional and mature influence in your style. Think of the all-powerful Mountain, towering above you, unbothered by your feeble attempts to conquer it. Imagine Mountain as the awe-inspiring, sublime elements in nature, like the cliff-edge in Wordsworth's poem *The Prelude*, a muscular horse running in the wind, a deep cavern at the depths of the ocean, or a lion gazing upon his lands. Mountain in nature is where the power lies.

When paired with other Style Roots, Mountain will often formalise it. The Mountain Style Root adds a professional or even stereotypically masculine quality. Masculine clothing tends to refer to styles that are more closely or exclusively associated with male wearers either in the present or in history. For example, suits, oversized shapes, structured pieces, trousers, waistcoats, ties, t-shirts; even jeans were largely worn first by men, and so they still have this masculine association. These items of clothing are also often more 'yang' (page 220), meaning sharp, tailored, structured and narrow. Someone with the Mountain Style Root will often bring these styles into an outfit, as well as professional 'feminine' items like pencil skirts, blouses and pointed heels.

Some words associated with the Mountain Style Root include:

- authoritative
- career-woman
- dignified
- expensive
- formal
- mature
- polished
- powerful
- presentable
- professional
- smart
- strong
- structured
- tailored

> It is hard to evade the idea of masculine and feminine, and we often use yin/yang within the style community as it much more closely attacks this idea of opposition and how opposites express themselves; however, sometimes I will use more gendered language when it helps to explain a concept.

The Mountain will feel comforting because of their strength. They are unwavering when they know they are right, and will fight for what they believe in. They have the feeling of a businesswoman, even if they don't work in an office in a New York skyscraper. They lead the way at home or in friendships, keeping everybody organised. A simple chat with them will make you feel motivated, as though you can achieve anything you put your mind to. They can seem intimidating at first, as they can appear undaunted by the challenges of the world, or rather encourage them, tackling them head-on, and will help you to do the same.

Elements in clothing or outfits that make them Mountain:

Your outfit may have two or more of these elements to make it Mountain, and certainly not all of them.

Suit elements

You do not have to wear a classic three-piece suit to qualify as someone with the Mountain Style Root, but traditional suit/office-wear items will often find their way into your outfits. These include:

○ Structured coats

○ Blazers

○ Waistcoats

○ Suit trousers

○ Pencil skirts

○ Blouses

○ Button-down shirts

○ Ties/bow ties/structured collars

○ Suspenders/braces

○ Large laptop-sized bags/briefcases

○ Heels or pointed shoes

○ Brogues/loafers

Stiff/structured fabrics

Often in Mountain-influenced outfits, the fabric will not appear loose, draped or soft but stiff and strong. This can be achieved with fabrics like leather, stiff cotton or wool.

Quality fabrics

Mountain can have an element of luxury to it, so quality or expensive looking/feeling fabrics can be a simple way to add Mountain to an outfit. Mountain fabrics also tend to be smooth and clean rather than messy. These include:

○ Cotton

○ Wool

○ Silk

○ Cashmere

○ Leather

High necks

A higher neckline tends to add a feeling of sharpness, as well as modesty, to an outfit. A turtleneck, crew neck or collar, for example, will make an outfit feel more Mountain.

Collars

A collar is a simple way to infuse elements of the suit into an outfit without feeling too formal. Whether on a shirt or a dress, a collar (especially a button-down collar) will add a sense of formality and professionalism to any look.

Strong colour contrast

Mountain will often use neutral tones, much like Mushroom (page 25), to convey a sense of professional formality; however, rather than the blended feel of Mushroom, Mountain favours strength and power and so combines highly contrasted colours like black and white.

Oversized shapes

Long or large shapes continue the feeling of intimidation that sometimes comes with the Mountain Style Root. Whereas some Style Roots have a paired-back feel, Mountain is a root that adds to an outfit to give it that extra something.

Stone

Stone is the casual, relaxed, sporty, urban influence in your style. It represents the places of the world where we go to be active, to walk or simply hang out. A concrete path through the city, a pile of grey, jagged rocks on a hill or the pebbles on a beach are perfect examples of the influence of Stone in the real world. Stone is a beagle wandering a hiking trail, a playful monkey in the trees, or the lone fox pilfering snacks from people's trash in the city.

When paired with other Style Roots, Stone will often make an outfit more relaxed. It will add a casual tension to any outfit it encounters. Someone with the Stone Style Root might love to go to the gym in the city or backpack on hiking trails. Stone will add a dynamic messiness to any outfit.

Stone can be resilient yet also at peace. They are happy making their own way through the world in a very physical way. They might like to play sports and prefer going for long walks over taking the bus, or they might be the opposite and be very happy lounging about on the sofa at a friend's house. Those with the Stone Style Root are not particularly influenced by seeming impressive to others, although they might like to feel 'cool' or appear as relaxed about the world as they feel on the inside.

Some words
associated with the
Stone Style Root
include:

- athletic
- casual
- industrial
- messy
- practical
- relaxed
- slouched
- sporty
- urban
- utilitarian

Elements in clothing or outfits that make them Stone:

Your outfit may have two or more of these elements to make it Stone, and certainly not all of them.

Sportswear or athleisure styles

You don't need to dress like you are going to the gym to dress Stone, but some of these elements might add a more relaxed, down-to-earth feel to your style. These include:

○ Puffer coat

○ Boiler suits

○ Leggings

○ Cycling shorts

○ Tennis skirt

○ Jerseys

○ Hoodies/sweatshirts

○ T-shirts

○ Polo shirts

○ Sports bras/tops

○ Trainer socks

○ Trainers (including running trainers, converse, chunky trainers, fashion-led trainers, anything with laces)

○ Bum bags

○ Caps

○ Sunglasses

○ Graphic prints/ brand names

Oversized/baggy/chunky shapes

- These kinds of silhouette convey the 'I don't really care' feel that Stone really thrives in.

- For example, an oversized blazer takes itself a lot less literally than a blazer that is fitted and neat. There is a sloppy element infused into the item that makes it feel a lot more Stone.

- A chunky pair of boots has a much more practical feel than something sleek or dainty.

- A baggy, slouchy pair of jeans is easier to put on the body and move in than something stiff and structured, so gives a practical, Stone feel to an outfit.

Distressed fabrics

- Denim (especially acid or light wash)

- Plastic-based fabrics such as polyester

- Fleece

- Canvas

- Linen

- Mesh

Tension-building details

- Frayed edges

- Zips

- Shoelaces

- Hoods

- Oversized pockets

Sporty prints

- Checkerboard

- Patchwork

Earth

Earth is the natural, flowing, grounded Style Root and is the root most closely associated with the outdoors. In nature, Earth is the soft soil, untouched weeds, and daisies popping through the grass in spring. Earth expresses itself as the mulched autumn leaves in the woods or toads hopping into the pond. It is nature at its deepest point, near and under the ground.

When combined with other Style Roots, an Earth influence makes an outfit feel freer and loosens up the clothing, making it more relaxed and at ease. Earth may also make an outfit feel rougher and take it away from the modern world towards a more grounded identity.

Someone with the Earth Style Root is very in touch with the natural world. They might have an interest in animals, categorising plants, or simply enjoy looking up at the clouds. They often have a penchant for vintage, and their home might be littered with knick-knacks picked up from antique stores.

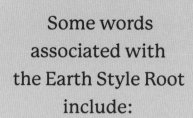

Some words associated with the Earth Style Root include:

- academic
- bohemian
- country
- eclectic
- effortless
- flowing
- grounded
- natural
- outdoors
- relaxed
- rough
- rugged

Stone cares deeply about the state of the world and often becomes passionate when a topic veers towards one of their interests. They trust their gut and are not afraid to engage in their hobbies. They frequently enjoy learning in all forms, whether academic or practical. They are keen to use their hands and get stuck in.

Elements in clothing or outfits that make them Earth:

Your outfit may have two or more of these elements to make it Earth, and certainly not all of them.

Natural fabrics

Fabrics that looked like they were pulled from the wilderness are the best for Earth lovers. This means natural, rough, coarse or worn fabrics.

- Linen
- Cotton
- Leather
- Fluff
- Fur
- Fleece
- Flannel
- Corduroy
- Denim
- Waffle textures
- Wool
- Tweed
- Wood (such as a wooden bangle)
- Suede
- Animal print/skin. Of course, this can sometimes create tension with people who have the Earth Style Root, as they often also care deeply about the natural world and shopping and dressing sustainably and ethically. The production of natural fabrics can be just as complex as the production of synthetic fabrics, but if you prefer, do seek out faux leather, faux snakeskin, faux fluff/fur, and try to shop second-hand to embrace your Earth root while avoiding overproduction.

Loose, flowing fabrics

Wide legs and bell sleeves are the kinds of shapes you would expect to see in Earth. Depending on what Earth is paired with, it may also express itself in oversized shapes like trench coats or baggy trousers.

Bohemian patterns

Patterns that originate from natural practices (rather than feeling graphic or machine-created) tend to give a very natural, Earth feel.

Mid-century, retro and vintage elements

○ Earth is the Style Root most likely to explore styles of the past. Up until recently, most fabrics and clothing items were not made with plastic or mass-produced using machines, so they have a certain natural quality.

○ The 1970s, in particular, is an influence for Earth-lovers as it was the origin of the popular bohemian aesthetic. The 1960s is also great for psychedelic-inspired Earth looks. A hint of any era of history in an outfit will create an Earth impression.

Practical accessories

Anything you would need to wear outdoors to protect yourself from the elements would be completely appropriate in an Earth context. This includes:

○ Raincoats

○ Fleece/parka jacket

○ Gilet

○ Jeans

○ Sunglasses

○ Sunhats (including floppy hats, caps and bucket hats)

○ Hiking boots

○ Wellington boots

○ Cowboy boots

Natural colour palette

Colours with natural tones have an Earth-like feel to them – any colours you might find regularly outside. These include:

○ Shades of green

○ Shades of brown

○ Rust/copper tones

○ Aubergine

- Oranges and yellows
- Deep reds
- Teal
- Shades of grey
- Sky blue

Layering

Layering creates a deconstructed vibe and adds to the 'un-done' feeling of Earth, mirroring how the natural world is rarely clean-cut. Think layered necklaces, multiple jackets, or tops layered under shirts.

Flower

Flower is the intricate, delicate, dainty influence in your style. Imagine a growing blossom, gentle to the touch, small and light. In nature, Flower expresses itself as a bee bumbling from bush to bush, a butterfly fluttering its wings in the sun, a baby rabbit hopping on the grass or a puffy cloud drifting across the skyline.

When Flower is added to an outfit, it becomes more light, airy and delicate. This Style Root is the closest aligned to the stereotypical associations with the words 'feminine' or 'girly' and draws from shapes and items associated with traditionally girly spheres or pursuits like ballet, baking or strawberry picking. As a Style Root, Flower is focused on the miniscule, cute and light delights in life. The Flower influence creates a sensitive, sweet feel.

Someone with the Flower Style Root is soft in every way. They are respectful of the thoughts and feelings of others and very empathic. They have a young, kind spirit and are very generous with their smiles. They might be attracted to vintage items like hairbrushes or jewellery boxes from the 1950s, enjoy flower-arranging or baking a pie. They might still keep soft toys in their home or dress their plates with pretty napkins.

Some words
associated with the
Flower Style Root
include:

- charming
- dainty
- delicate
- dreamy
- elegant
- ethereal
- feminine
- flowing
- graceful
- intricate
- Parisian
- pastel
- princess
- rounded
- soft
- vintage
- whimsical
- youthful

Flower would happily wander the streets of Paris with a basket on their arm full of macaroons and raspberry jam. Don't be mistaken into thinking that it is only young girls who can have the Flower Style Root. Lots of women worry about looking 'frumpy' or older by drawing on girlish styles, but with a few tweaks, Flower can remain a sophisticated way to express yourself as you age.

Elements in clothing or outfits that make them Flower:

Your outfit may have two or more of these elements to make it Flower, and certainly not all of them.

Ribbons and bows

Delicate, round, little shapes on an outfit usually denote Flower in some way – and bows and ribbons are all these things! They are also associated with girlhood and youthful femininity (as little girls' hair is often tied up in bows).

Lace and embroidery

○ Any kind of lace, whether it's a very intricate or broderie anglaise, will add a touch of Flower to an outfit.

○ Delicate embroidery created with needle and thread will add a feeling of care to an outfit.

Princess silhouettes

Any shapes associated with fairy tales or princess silhouettes are very sentimental and create a Flower feel. These include:

○ Bardot sleeves

○ Off-the-shoulder neckline

○ Delicate straps

○ Flared skirt (especially with a rounded shape)

○ Nipped-in waist

Pastel tones

Pink, of course, has a significant Flower influence. It is closely associated with femininity societally and has a lightness and softness that matches the Flower Style Root. However, other pastel or light tones, including beige and cream, as well as sky blue and lemon yellow, will add a very Flower vibe to an outfit.

Vintage inspiration

Traditionally, women have worn very delicate clothing across the decades, so pulling from the past will often increase the Flower feel in an outfit. Whether it's the delicate petticoats of the 1950s, corsets reminiscent of the 18th-century, headbands from the 1920s or simply fabrics that have been consistently used across fashion eras, like cotton and lace.

Fluffy and soft fabrics

Fluffy shapes tend to be round and delicate so are complementary to the Flower. These can include:

○ Sheepskin-style jackets

○ Fur coats

○ Chiffon

○ Feathers

Small delicate patterns

A small, light-hearted print will create a sense of delicate intricacy. Some examples of this include:

○ Gingham

○ Some plaids

Floral motifs

Whether introduced in pattern, print or 3D elements, of course it wouldn't be the Flower Style Root if Flowers were not involved! Feel free to be a little meta with this one.

Celestial motifs

Another side of Flower is the light, angelic influence it has. Stars, Moons and sparkle motifs can all create a delicate, feminine, Flower feel.

Fire

Fire is the sensual, glamorous, passionate influence in your style. Imagine a flame, it radiates a warm, intoxicating glow. In nature, the Fire Style Root expresses itself as a rolling thunderstorm with a crack of rain, a tropical rainforest lush with colour and heat, a tiger prowling through the greenery, or a low, burnt orange sunset painted across a still lake.

Fire adds a glamorous, luxurious feel and makes an outfit more lavish, soft, and romantic. Don't be mistaken into thinking that Fire is all about being sexy or revealing. How much skin you do or do not show might play a small role in the effect of an outfit, but there is so much more to Fire than this. Fire is a woman sipping a martini under her floppy hat on a yacht in St Tropez or a mythical queen dripping in jewels. I also often associate the Fire Style Root with certain traditional Spanish or Italian fashions, especially dancing dresses with peplums, and red lips.

Someone with the Fire Style Root is alluring and captivating and makes the people around them feel confident in themselves, inspired for life. They might enjoy the finer things in life and know how to have fun, but just as passion can be romantic, it can also generate anger and rage: Fire feels things deeply and is intense with their emotions.

Some words associated with the Fire Style Root include:

- alluring
- commanding
- enticing
- glamorous
- lavish
- lush
- luxurious
- opulent
- passionate
- powerful
- romantic
- royal
- sensual
- sexy
- smoky
- sultry

Elements in clothing or outfits that make them Fire:

Your outfit may have two or more of these elements to make it Fire, and certainly not all of them.

Figure-hugging silhouettes

Fire can be emphasised by physicality. This does not mean that this is the only way to create the Fire effect, but it is worth noting that figure-enhancing shapes can play a role in increasing the level of Fire in an outfit. Some examples include:

○ Nipped-in waists (a pencil skirt is the perfect example of this, creating a cinched effect at the top and bottom of the garment)

○ Sweetheart necklines

○ Ruched fabrics

○ Wrap details

Sparkle or glitter

Sparkle or glitter (used in a punchier way than the delicate sparkle of the Flower Style Root) adds a glamorous feel to an outfit. Much like a mirror ball, the Fire Style Root is not afraid to attract attention and shine.

Heels

Discomfort is by no means necessary if you have the Fire Style Root; but if you would like to make an impact, heels are a great way to do it. Unlike the Mountain Style Root, where a pair of flats can be enhanced with a pointed toe, with Fire it isn't the sharpness of the shoe that gives impact, but the height. Wedges have the same effect, or even a pair of wedged trainers, so don't feel like you have to wear stilettos all the time!

Large, round accessories

○ Large round sunglasses

○ Floppy hat

○ Pendants

○ Draped jewelled necklaces

○ Gold bangles

○ Chunky rings

○ Oversized handbag

Animal print

Exotic animals, such as the jaguar, tiger, cheetah or lion, have a fierce attitude, much like the Fire root. When you dress in their pattern, you take on an element of their energy.

Jewels

A key word of Fire is 'opulence'. A jewellery box overflowing with pearls and diamonds is a dream for someone with the Fire Style Root. Whether worn as a necklace, on a handbag or a shoe, or subtle diamantes on a dress, jewels show your taste for the lavish things in life.

Lace

The delicate intricacy of lace is often associated with lingerie and nightwear, so can add a sensual and womanly effect to an outfit.

Fur

Historically, fur was expensive and glamorous, so it is inherently Fire. Some of the Style Roots are about paring things down: Fire is not one of them, and wearing fur matches this energy. The soft, round, exaggerated shape of fur also naturally lends itself to the Fire Style Root. Sourcing both fur and faux fur sustainably is difficult, even impossible. I suggest shopping second hand if this is an aspect of Fire that you enjoy and want to bring into your wardrobe.

Red tones

The colour red has a strong psychological association with passion. Red is, of course, one of the colours of flames, the sunset and a universal symbol for danger. Our brains take note of the colour red, and so wearing this colour shows you are happy for people to stop and stare.

Silk

Silk is a soft, luxurious fabric, associated with nighties as well as evening gowns and feminine luxury.

Lingerie or lingerie-inspired

The trend of layering corsets, bras and stockings can certainly be utilised in a Fire context.

Velvet

Velvet and similar soft, plush fabrics are associated with luxury and can therefore be used to great effect with the Fire root.

Royalty-inspired

There is something royal about the
Fire Style Root: lush deep purples,
jewels and fur. Imagine a crown
atop the head of a fantasy queen
or the cape around her shoulders.
Precious fabrics feel important and
should be introduced to your outfits
in some way.

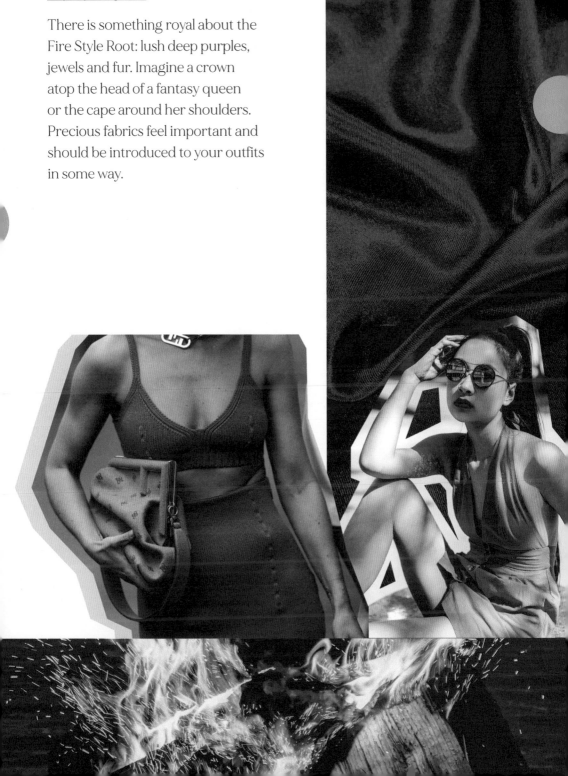

Moon

Moon is the dark, edgy, gloomy, emotional influence in your style. Moon is the endless dark night sky studded with stars and dusty grey clouds, it is the shadow in the corner of your eye, the wilting, thorned rose, a wolf stalking its prey and bones on the forest floor.

In combination with other Style Roots, Moon adds a dark or ethereal feel to an outfit, making it moodier and more intense. When paired with Stone, the result is seen through traditional punk elements like chunky leather boots; when paired with Fire, you get leopard print and lace; when paired with Earth, certain rockstar elements are introduced to an outfit. There is an iteration of Moon for almost all the other Style Roots; it acts as a subversion – a kind of 'upside down'. You can think of it as putting the other Style Roots in a minor key. As such, Moon styles often feel vampiric, ghostly, wolfish or witchy.

Someone with the Moon Style Root is dark and emotional. Outwardly, they can appear intimidating; they might scowl, roll their eyes and have a general aura of indifference. However, underneath they feel pain and sadness deeply and will spend time ruminating on their feelings.

Some words associated with the Moon Style Root include:

- celestial
- daring
- dark
- deep
- edgy
- ethereal
- gothic
- grunge
- haunting
- intense
- moody
- mysterious
- mystical
- nightfall
- rebellious
- sharp
- strong
- witchy

Elements in clothing or outfits that make them Moon:

Your outfit may have two or more of these elements to make it Moon, and certainly not all of them.

Dark colour palette

- **Black:** This will add a Moon element to any outfit. Black is the simplest symbol of the night: the darkness, the emptiness, the shadows. In the West especially, black is a symbol of death and is traditionally worn to funerals.

- **White:** Conversely, as much as black can be Moon-ish, so can white. There is a ghostliness or ethereal quality added to an outfit when white is used.

- **Other dark shades:** Grey, dark green, red or purple.

- **Brown:** Because brown has warmth to its tone, it is actually the hardest to create a 'Moon' feel with it. Cooler brown tones work best.

Leather

Leather is traditionally associated with adventure. Leather came into fashion when motorcycle and aviator jackets became common, both of which are associated with dangerous and rebellious activities.

Feminine vintage styles

The past is a fascination to those with the Moon Style Root. Where there is an exploration of the past, there is an exploration of death, and so elements of vintage style become a symbol of the passage of time. Play with things like:

- Corsets

- Lace

- Tulle

Crosses

Bram Stoker's novel *Dracula* is the most famous example of a piece of gothic literature that took Christian imagery to the dark side. The TV series *Buffy the Vampire Slayer* is a great example of how a simple crucifix added to an outfit can act as a symbol of darkness. The easiest way to introduce this is via jewellery.

Velvet

Velvet is reminiscent of vampiric imagery; it is a subversion of the royal themes of the Fire Style Root – that powerful energy becoming polluted by darkness.

Tattoos

This is, of course, by no means a mandatory requisite of creating a Moon feel in your style, as it is very permanent. However, tattoos have long been associated with dark, edgy aesthetics for a few reasons. Firstly, the pain element; the fact that the wearer chooses to undergo a lengthy, teeth-gritting experience shows their penchant for the darker side of life. Secondly, they are often dark in colour or theme. Not everyone with tattoos will have a Moon Style Root but it is a factor to consider.

Animal

As much as leopards, snakes and cheetahs are seductive and smooth, they are also dangerous. This is why we see animal print in both the Fire and Moon Style Roots.

Stripes

In nature, stripes are used to signal danger. Whether on a wasp or a tiger, these shapes say, 'fear me'.

Chains

Via bags, belts or necklaces, chains are an easy accessory to add to an outfit to create a Moon feel. Chains are hard, made of strong metal and are often associated with prisons (mental or physical) and pain.

Ripped elements

Ripped jeans are symbolic of fearless and reckless action.

Studs

These hard, threatening shapes say, 'stay away from me, I am dangerous', and can be added to clothes, a bag or a pair of shoes. If your outfit looks like it could do some damage, then it securely sits in the Moon Style Root.

Plaid

You need look no further than Vivienne Westwood to understand the importance of plaid to the Moon Style Root. Plaid found its groove in

Britain with the edgy styles of the punk movement in the 1970s, and so plaid will forever be associated with this rebellious era.

Astrology

As much as the Moon Style Root embodies darkness, there are also glimmers of light. Taking literal inspiration from the night sky in the form of star patterns or moon motifs can add to the Moon feel. This also acts as another subversion of the Flower Style Root.

Sun

Sun is the fun, playful and experimental Style Root. In nature, Sun is the rainforest – red and green macaws swooping through orchids and tropical trees. It is oranges swelling on their branches, the blue of the ocean against hot sand, the rich red of maple trees or a bee landing on an open, yellow flower.

When combined with other Style Roots, Sun adds a bold and unusual feel. Don't assume that because you enjoy having fun with fashion that you have the Sun Style Root; you can love layering, thrifting and expanding your boundaries without being Sun. When Sun is added to an outfit it becomes more extreme; the sleeves get larger, the structure becomes harsher, the lace gets lacier. Often Sun is colourful and bright – but not always. You may find details where you might not expect them, like zips where a hem should be, menswear combined with womenswear, frills mixed in with sportswear. The street style aesthetic, for example, often incorporates Sun elements, especially during fashion weeks across the world. Sun can also manifest in a certain silliness – through graphic tees or novelty trainers – and often employs ironic details.

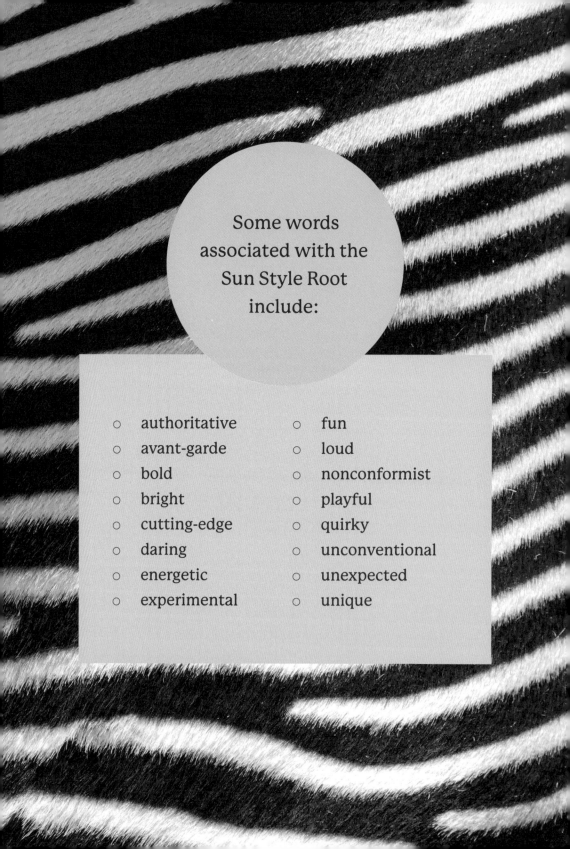

Some words associated with the Sun Style Root include:

- authoritative
- avant-garde
- bold
- bright
- cutting-edge
- daring
- energetic
- experimental
- fun
- loud
- nonconformist
- playful
- quirky
- unconventional
- unexpected
- unique

Someone with the Sun Style Root is cheeky and playful. They might have a child-like whimsy and they're not afraid to subvert expectations of their character. They are often witty, comedic and like to be challenged. They are not afraid to have a debate and are likely to win it. They are experimental, and simultaneously impulsive, leading to an array of both finished and unfinished projects. They are fundamentally curious about how things work and why we make the decisions we do, and they want to carve their own path.

Elements in clothing or outfits that make them Sun:

Your outfit may have two or more of these elements to make it Sun, and certainly not all of them.

Bright colours

The easiest way to create the Sun effect in your outfit is to add a pop of colour. A bright colour is one with high chroma, so it is closer to clear than to grey – it should feel shocking to the eye. Christmas red, hot pink and electric blue are all examples of bright colours. Some of you will be turned off from the Sun Style Root on this basis alone, so know that this is not a must-have element of the style – the fact that you don't like bright colours doesn't necessarily mean you aren't Sun! With that said, moments of colour are an easy signal to the eye that you are unafraid to dress outside the box.

Unexpected colours

Brightness isn't the only way to use colour to make an outfit feel Sun. Adding colour where you wouldn't expect it is another way to channel the Sun Style Root. Wearing a yellow pair of heels with a neutral outfit or a red belt with an all-black outfit adds a pop of colour where you might expect a neutral. Similarly, wearing a pastel pink pair of chunky combat boots has the same effect; the softness of the pastel contradicts the destructive energy of the shoe.

Monochrome

Monochrome can appear very Mushroom which is essentially the opposite of Sun, so it is strange to think that it also applies here. But in fact, monochrome is an extreme detail, so an outfit swathed in one colour can feel over-the-top or 'unnecessary', creating that ironic Sun feel.

Bold patterns

A zebra print, chevron or oversized polka dot is instantly eye-catching.

Pattern mixing or clashing

When combining a leopard print jacket with a plaid skirt it can be a challenge not to look like a five-year-old who has raided her mum's wardrobe – but this is almost the point when it comes to the Sun Style Root. Pairing a polka dot with a stripe is a simple way to say, 'I don't really care about your traditional fashion rules' (the Sun always does her own thing). The most effective way to mix patterns is to find a connection – either the colours or the size of the motif should be the same or similar.

High contrast

When the items in an outfit contradict each other, this is contrast. It could be as simple as wearing a black top and white trousers – these colours are opposites and so there is an exciting, jarring energy when they are paired together. Contrasting very feminine pieces with very masculine pieces has a similar effect.

Unusual or extreme textures

Textures that you wouldn't expect to find in clothing are the most interesting, so futuristic or inventive fabrics like metals or plastics can feel very Sun. Similarly, employing fabrics where you wouldn't expect to find them can have the same effect, for example, a puffed sleeve made of leather is an exciting contradiction. Extreme textures literally mean taking a texture to its extreme – so rather than a little sparkle, the dress is completely made of sequins.

Extreme shapes

When an item feels unnecessarily big or small this creates questions; primarily, 'why?'. Sun is not practically focused in its motivation, so having oversized sleeves, ridiculously chunky heels or a tiny handbag is appealing to them in its ironic uselessness.

Details in unusual places

Irony and misusing details is very
Sun - for example, having bows
where buttons would be far more
effective.

Avant-garde influence

Any details that are futuristic
or are a modern reimagining
of a previous style or trend
feel very Sun.

Choosing your Style Roots

You are not two-dimensional

Hopefully, some of those Style Roots resonated with you. If you feel that not every characteristic of your favourite Style Root applied to you, or some of the characteristics of a different root applied to you, this is a good thing! The point of Style Roots is not to funnel you into one specific style. You might read about distinct styles you feel you have to choose from – bohemian, girly, edgy and so on – but, actually, the people with the best style incorporate a mix of influences to end up with something original and unique. It might help to look at the personalities of each Style Root and mull over if you see yourself within them; you will never *only* be sweet or funny or emotional – the key parts of your identity might be a combination of all three.

Three is the perfect number

You might feel there is a little piece of you in each of the eight Style Roots, and that's okay. I love aspects of each – when I am creating Pinterest boards or finding outfits for clients, I often have to put myself in the headspace of each of the roots and find a true appreciation and excitement for each.

However, a wardrobe with eight different core influences can feel a little messy and incohesive. It is much harder to pull out any two pieces of clothing and find a story that pulls both pieces together and makes sense with your style. Similarly, an outfit with loads of different influences doesn't say anything about you – when you try to embrace every style, you end up with no style at all.

Here are a few examples that demonstrate how your personal style is more than just a mere aesthetic. By combining three Style Roots you'll find so many ways to express yourself through clothes.

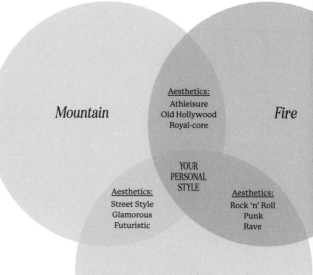

Mountain

Fire

Aesthetics:
Athleisure
Old Hollywood
Royal-core

YOUR
PERSONAL
STYLE

Aesthetics:
Street Style
Glamorous
Futuristic

Aesthetics:
Rock 'n' Roll
Punk
Rave

Sun

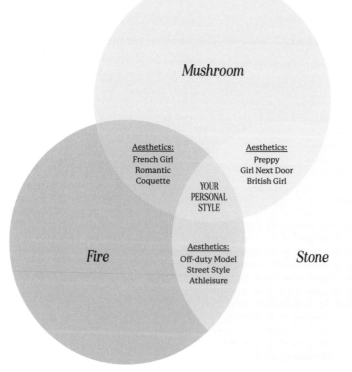

Mushroom

Aesthetics:
French Girl
Romantic
Coquette

Aesthetics:
Preppy
Girl Next Door
British Girl

YOUR
PERSONAL
STYLE

Fire

Aesthetics:
Off-duty Model
Street Style
Athleisure

Stone

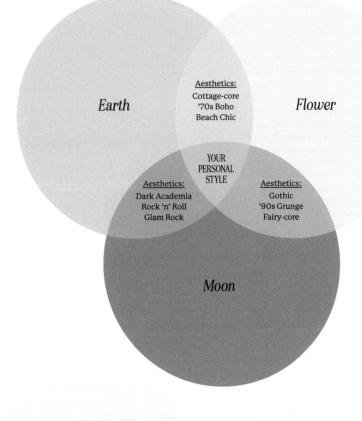

Earth

Flower

Aesthetics:
Cottage-core
'70s Boho
Beach Chic

YOUR
PERSONAL
STYLE

Aesthetics:
Dark Academia
Rock 'n' Roll
Glam Rock

Aesthetics:
Gothic
'90s Grunge
Fairy-core

Moon

Stone

Aesthetics:
Old Money
Beach Chic
Ballet-core

Aesthetics:
Nautical
Scandi Girl
Athleisure

YOUR
PERSONAL
STYLE

Aesthetics:
Old Hollywood
Light Academia
Royal-core

Flower

Mountain

I find three Style Roots to be the perfect number to work with. With only one or two Style Roots guiding your wardrobe, your style will be cohesive but also stereotypical and predictable. For example, if you focus on just the Moon Style Root, it will feel like you are wearing an emo costume rather than expressing your personal style; if you only focus on the Flower Style Root, you will look like you are dressing up as a little girl. Even with two Style Roots you are limited – Flower and Moon paired is simply the gothic aesthetic; Mushroom and Mountain paired is just office style. Have a look at the diagrams on page 74 to see a few examples of this Style Root interaction – when you introduce a third Style Root it actually allows you to play with fashion and take your style beyond just a mere aesthetic.

Most people struggle to narrow down to three Style Roots from four. I cannot stop you from focusing on four roots – ultimately you must do what feels right for you – but I find four Style Roots to feel unfocused. When you follow four roots, it is much harder to find all of them in one item of clothing and it will be more tempting to give up and buy imperfect pieces.

Having three Style Roots is both unique and streamlined. You have a strong foundation in two Style Roots, and your third root adds a unique edge to your combination.

Style Roots = style values

So, do you have to give up a piece of your identity to achieve a streamlined style? There is a part of you in each of the eight Style Roots, but the three you resonate with the most are the ones you should focus on.

Think of this exercise in a similar manner to choosing your core values. A quick Google search will reveal several lists about 200 words long from which you can choose your values. These values are the guiding forces for your life, and narrowing down can provide a checklist for next time you have an important decision to make. As much as sustainability, friendship and stability are important to me, in a crunch I will instinctively prioritise development, connection and adventure. There are many words on the core values list I feel I should choose, but are they actually what I value when it comes down to it? I want health to be one of my values, but if I must choose between finishing this chapter or going to the gym, I will choose writing again and again because, at my core, my motivations for writing it (development) are deeper to me. Try to be strict with yourself and select your three core Style Roots in the same way.

I have had quite a journey with my own Style Roots. Originally, I thought my roots were Mushroom, Flower and Fire, as I particularly love the 'French girl aesthetic'. After experimenting with this train of thought for about six months, I realised the glamour and sensuality of Fire actually don't feel very important to my wardrobe and outfit choices. I pondered that my third Style Root might be Sun as I have always loved being inventive with my style. After playing with that for a little while, I realised that although I love experimenting and subversion, it was nature that I treasured. I grew up in the countryside, in rural Norfolk in the UK, and it is the motifs of this environment that I find most joyful. When I looked back, I realised that it was the wicker baskets and

tweed blazers of the French girl aesthetic that I found exciting, far more so than sexy blouses and pops of red. I felt in tune with the retro influences of the style more than I liked patterns or bright colours. That's how I landed on Mushroom, Flower and Earth as my three core Style Roots. I do consider both Sun and Fire the adjacent Style Roots to my core trio – and sometimes you will see them seep into an outfit – but at my core it is Mushroom, Flower and Earth where I feel most comfortable and excited. All of this is to say that it's okay not to get your Style Roots correct straight away. I would never recommend buying an entire wardrobe of new clothes once you have decided your Style Roots because sometimes it takes a little time to settle in. Saying you should know your style overnight is like saying you should know yourself overnight.

Your Style Roots are more than descriptors of your style. They are your core motivators. There are times in my life where I could describe my style as edgy, boho, girly, sporty, relaxed, casual, colourful, professional *and* dark!

But if I look a little closer, I can see a deeper drive for simplicity, femininity and natural influences across formal situations, work events, parties and even walks in the woods. There are days where I want to experiment with rockstar outfits, cowboy looks, festival styles and professional styles, which is fine, but the key is approaching these outfits through the lens of your three core Style Roots. It makes for an exciting challenge! For example, for Halloween I might try to pick a costume that feels authentic to my Style Roots (in my case, dressing as an angel rather than the devil) as it would be exciting and fun to go the extremes of what my Style Roots might look like (and a bonus of this is that I would probably be able to reuse those clothes again!). You can view these moments as challenges, experiments or exercises to expand and reinvent your Style Roots.

Often, I hear some variation of the following:

I want to feel Mountain at work, I want to dress Fire when I go on a date, but I want to dress Stone when I am sitting at home.

Of course, you want to feel professional in a work setting, you want to feel unguarded and relaxed when you are at a family gathering and you want to look sexy when you go on a date. The key is to do this within your Style Roots. If you follow outside forces for your style, you'll need a different wardrobe for each occasion; a work wardrobe, a going-out wardrobe, a sitting at home wardrobe. This was how I shopped for a long time: buying a going-out dress for each new party, a new suit for a job interview or sets of sweats for sitting at home. The problem with this is that, firstly, it costs more money as you need more things to serve different purposes.

And, secondly, in none of these different instances are you dressing for yourself, so there is no joy in it. Last year, I wore a sexy red dress to a party and, as much as my body looked great, I looked at the dress afterwards and realised I would never wear it again. I wanted to make an impact, but in doing so I just looked like every other girl there rather than standing out as myself. Now, I have a different 'sexy dress' – it still looks great on my body but also says something about who I am through the colours and patterns it uses, and it has a level of modesty that feels more authentic to me and my core Style Roots. When you walk into your office, you don't want to look like a corporate drone. The cool thing about an office environment is it only takes a small change to convey your Style Roots, like carrying a pink bag, adding a quirky pair of earrings or wearing a tweed blazer. The benefit of focusing on your Style Roots for all aspects of your life is that the clothes in your wardrobe become interchangeable – you can wear your work blazer with your dinner dress and there is still a connection there. So, I'm not saying you should throw caution to the wind and wear your cottage-core dresses to the office, because that's clearly unrealistic, but there should be something of all three of your Style Roots in all the outfits you wear, everywhere.

Your style should say something deeper about who you are. As much as I think you can pick your Style Roots based on aesthetics, personality and values should also be a major factor. If you don't feel like you want to be glamorous and sensual, but you like the Fire Style Root on other people, it probably still isn't the right Style Root for you. It helps to look at what doesn't change about your style. Across the years, my favourite outfits have always been delicate, intricate, timeless, nostalgic, and earthy. It is okay to experiment, to try something different some days, but your Style Roots are what you come back to, to help prevent spontaneous purchases of items that will never again see the light of day. Your style is a key component of your personal brand and identity, and when it is congruent with your personality, you feel the most confident.

Decoding your Style Roots

You can choose your Style Roots

You might instantly feel drawn instinctively to three Style Roots, and that's great! You've found the easy route. Often, your gut instinct is the most important thing to follow. But if you're feeling stuck or unsure, I have a few techniques and exercises that will help you to settle on your three core Style Roots.

When choosing your Style Roots, it's important to consider the following: (These prompts can apply to outfits from the past and present)

○ How your style has changed over time.

○ Styles you come back to repeatedly.

○ The elements of your style that don't change.

○ Phases you had that in hindsight were failed experiments and not representative of your style.

○ Your favourite outfits and the reasons you like them (remember to try to be specific about these reasons).

○ Outfits that you feel most comfortable in.

○ Outfits that make you feel confident, powerful, sexy or beautiful.

○ Outfits you are proud of.

○ Outfits that represent something deeper about your identity and and the message you want to put out to the world.

○ What does the version of your best self look like? What is she doing with her life? What is she wearing? Try to look at yourself objectively.

Make notes based on these prompts then compare that information to each of the Style Roots (page 22) to see which roots match your style identity (or aspirational style identity) best.

For most people, the first and second Style Roots they land on are their most dominant ones and seem to come quite easily. Where most people get stuck is the third Style Root – narrowing down from four to three or expanding from two to three can feel like a challenge.

Finding your third root takes deep knowledge of yourself and who you are – this will be a little easier if you are typically introspective, but don't worry if it feels a little cloudy to you.

Once you've made notes based on these prompts and reviewed all eight Style Roots, complete the Style Streams Exercise (page 82) and the Style Roots Quiz (page 84) to delve deeper.

Style Streams Exercise

Each of the Style Roots essentially represents a list of style descriptors — a collection of different style ideas that are connected. I think of these collections of words as 'streams' that will lead to your 'roots'.

STEP 1: Write a list of 20—30 words that describe your style

These can be words that describe a vibe, colour, shape, aesthetic or effect. Use all three prompts to help you.

Your Dream Self: imagine the best version of yourself (but not an alternative lifestyle). Think about what she does for work, what she does to relax, and the kinds of friends she has.

○ How does she dress?

○ How would you describe her personality and lifestyle?

Your Wardrobe: what clothes do you have currently that you ...

○ Wear frequently

○ Truly love

Mood board: (if you don't use Pinterest, create one now!) after mood boarding outfits and pieces you love, describe the clothes you see.

STEP 2: Find connections between the words in your list

Using a highlighter, sort your words into groups. Don't worry too much at this point about making them fit into Style Roots criteria, just follow your instinct on which words seem to link naturally together. For example, 'Parisian' connects with 'vintage' and 'powerful' connects with 'structured'.

STEP 3: Organise your words into lists

Rewrite your words into their respective groups so that you can look at the groups individually. Try to pick a header word from each list that encapsulates the rest. If you have four to seven different lists, see if the words in your smaller lists actually fit somewhere within a bigger list (if not, question if they really have a strong presence in your style). The aim is to group and narrow your words down into three lists.

STEP 4: Match your lists with the Style Roots

Now review your three lists through the lens of the Style Roots (page 22). Which Style Root pairs best and describes each of your lists? Look carefully at the keywords used to describe each Style Root to find the closest matches.

Example: My Style Roots Exercise

Here is my own list of words based on my dream self, my current wardrobe and things that appeal to me on my mood board. I've grouped the words into three lists, then matched a Style Root to each list.

Group 1 (Flower Style Root)	Group 2 (Mushroom Style Root)	Group 3 (Earth Style Root)
○ Bright	○ Audrey Hepburn	○ Academic
○ Delicate	○ Calm	○ Adventurous
○ Friendly	○ Classic	○ British
○ Fun	○ Elegant	○ Cool
○ Girlfriend	○ Mature	○ Countryside
○ Girl-next-door	○ Neutrals	○ Cowgirl
○ Innocent	○ Powerful	○ Eclectic
○ Inspiring	○ Put-together	○ Preppy
○ Parisian	○ Simple	○ Retro
○ Pink	○ Timeless	○ Rockstar
○ Sweet		○ Rural
○ Vintage		○ Safari
		○ Travel

This list is very personal, and some of it might seem nonsensical to someone else, but when you look at these words as a group it becomes clear why they are related. Some of the items on this list are slightly controversial: the imagined version of myself as the cute, sexy girlfriend across the table from my boyfriend might not be deemed by some as aspirational, or as something that should affect my style, but this is a vision of myself that I'm often excited by, and so it is honest to have it written there. Being vulnerable about who you are, about your dreams and your realities, is the only way to find yourself and therefore find your style.

Style Roots Quiz

When I first launched the idea of Style Roots to my social media followers, I did so with a version of this quiz. The aim is to help you focus on your deeper impulses and confirm your Style Roots once and for all. For each question, simply circle the answers that resonates with you most.

1. Which of these words do you feel most closely represents your personality? Think about who you are at your core and the elements that are consistent.

a. Understated
b. Competent
c. Eclectic
d. Easy-going
e. Rebellious
f. Quirky
g. Sweet
h. Sensual

2. Which of these fabrics do you find yourself most drawn to?

a. Cashmere
b. Cotton
c. Denim
d. Linen
e. Metallics
f. Leather
g. Silk
h. Lace
i. Sensual

3. In which of these locations would you feel most comfortable?

a. Empty beach
b. Busy office
c. Wild garden
d. City streets
e. Rainforest
f. Nightclub
g. Patisserie
h. Mansion

4. How would you most want people to describe you at a party?

a. Elegant
b. Smart
c. Free-spirited
d. Relaxed
e. Unusual
f. Mysterious
g. Graceful
h. Sexy

5. How would you most like your home to feel?

a. Neutral
b. Mature
c. Rugged
d. Industrial
e. Experimental
f. Haunting
g. Dreamy
h. Luxurious

6. How do/would you like to feel when dressing for work? (Forget about the rules of your specific workplace)

a. Timeless
b. Powerful
c. Grounded
d. Active
e. Fun
f. Daring
g. Charming
h. Glamorous

7. Which of these activities sounds the most enjoyable?

a. Observing modern art
b. Delivering an empowering speech
c. Walking in the forest
d. Playing tennis
e. Trying new foods in a market
f. Exploring an abandoned building
g. Attending afternoon tea
h. Drinking cocktails at a club

8. Which of these factors is most important to you when choosing a new bag?

a. Simple
b. Structured
c. Practical
d. Casual
e. Unique
f. Dark
g. Whimsical
h. Lavish

9. Which of these careers sounds most appealing to you?

a. Interior designer
b. Lawyer
c. Lifestyle blogger
d. Academic
e. Film producer
f. Song writer
g. Primary school teacher
h. Luxury goods marketeer

10. Which of these details do you feel most attracted to?

a. Plain
b. Pinstripe
c. Tweed
d. Argyle
e. Stripes
f. Studs
g. Floral
h. Leopard print

11. How would you most like your makeup to look on a first date?

a. Effortless
b. Polished
c. Natural
d. Sculpted
e. Bright
f. Dark
g. Soft
h. Smoky

12. Which of these design styles do you resonate with the most?

a. Minimalist
b. Professional
c. Bohemian
d. Preppy
e. Avant-garde
f. Gothic
g. Parisian
h. Glam

13. Which of these words would your close friends use to describe you?

a. Modest
b. Commanding
c. Flowing
d. Sporty
e. Deep
f. Dainty
g. Experimental
h. Alluring

If you mostly picked:

a — you are Mushroom
b — you are Mountain
c — you are Earth
d — you are Stone
e — you are Sun
f — you are Moon
g — you are Flower
h — you are Fire

Of course, you have three Style Roots, so you are looking for your top three most common letters!

By this point, you should feel confident in your three chosen Style Roots. I really do recommend implementing all three methods: reviewing the Style Roots (page 22), doing the Style Streams Exercise (page 82) and completing the Style Roots Quiz (page 84). Although you may come out with slightly different roots for the varying exercises, you should be able to find patterns that cement your decision. Doing the quiz at the end of the process often works like flipping a coin — if you're disappointed with the result, it reveals which Style Roots you most wanted to align with all along.

Combining your Style Roots

The 56 combinations

Your Style Roots don't exist in isolation. Unlike other style theories, the idea is not to box you into one narrow style like 'bohemian' or 'girly', because we are all more complicated than that. Your three Style Roots represent your three core motivations, or the three core elements of your personality that you want to express through your clothing.

There are 56 combinations of Style Roots. I see them as multiplied elements rather than additions. For example, I write my Style Roots as *Mushroom x Flower x Earth*. What this represents to me is that each of my Style Roots interacts with the others and should be present in each item of clothing or outfit I wear, as opposed to being separate elements that bump together. Essentially, your Style Roots affect each other; the way Earth shows up when combined with Mountain (an academic vibe) is different to the way it presents when combined with Sun (a bohemian festival feel) – we've already touched on this in the diagrams on page 74. You might have a gut negative reaction to one of the Style Roots because you have a one-dimensional view of it. It can help to reimagine that Style Root paired with a different Style Root to unlock its positives for you.

Can your Style Roots change?

I get this question a lot, and people often don't like my answer. On the one hand, I agree that we are fluid, that our style changes and grows with us, and so I understand the impulse to flip-flop between Style Roots. On the other hand, Style Roots are more than descriptors, they are the core motivations behind what we love to wear, and this shouldn't be influenced too much by external factors. The motivation behind Style Roots is to reduce what you buy, move away from trends, and follow a more authentic self that is more than just skin deep. Allowing yourself and your style to be swayed by whims or sudden trends won't help you to achieve this.

Of course, we grow and discover more about ourselves over time, and through this process we might unearth a Style Root we hadn't previously considered. I have re-evaluated my Style Roots a couple of times and moved from Fire to Sun and finally to Earth. However, I don't believe that my actual Style Roots ever changed – I just gained a better understanding of what they truly were. I love to experiment with style, and some days I might want to try an edgy outfit or a professional or quirky one, but this doesn't detract from my overall shopping and styling patterns.

What about seasonal changes?
Many people note that they feel their style change depending on the seasons. They typically feel more Flower in spring, Sun in summer, Earth in autumn and Moon in Winter. Again, I'd come back to my opinion that your style shouldn't be so strongly influenced by outward influences. Just as you wouldn't let trends each year move you strongly, don't let the weather or the vibes push you to extremes. That said, the order of your roots might change depending on which motivation feels strongest to you during that period. I allow myself to lean more on my Earth Style Root in autumn and lean more on Flower in spring, however I try not to stray too far from my other roots and would never abandon a root completely in one of my outfits. Dressing in tune with your Style Roots is essentially a centring exercise, a bit like meditation – you observe the impulses come and go, but choose to focus on your deeper, long-term joy.

Ordering your Style Roots

Does the order of your Style Roots matter? The shrewdest amongst you might notice that if you take order into account, there are *way* more than 56 unique combinations of Style Roots (a number that goes into the thousands).

You are likely to feel that your three Style Roots don't have equal dominance in your style – that is completely normal. For example, I feel Flower is first, Mushroom second and Earth third. The reason I don't stress over the order though, is that I think this ebbs and flows with every outfit, across the seasons, and across varying situations. I lean more towards my Mushroom influence in professional settings or meetings, Flower when I am seeing my boyfriend's family, and Earth when I am going to a party – but all three Style Roots will always feature in some way.

Having three Style Roots, and the freedom to play with their order, gives you space to experiment with different elements of yourself and your style on a daily basis. But this also provides enough restraint to give you the creativity you need to create good outfits and a cohesive wardrobe. I don't think there is any need to be as rigid as *'every outfit*

must have more Flower elements than Mushroom and Earth elements because it's my most dominant root' – that takes the fun out of it and makes it more of a maths problem than a getting-dressed solution.

Why Style Roots are not just aesthetics

The surge in the need to 'find your aesthetic' is a largely unhelpful way to view your personal style. Aesthetics like 'coquette', 'dark academia', 'mermaid-core' or even wider fashion movements like 'punk', '1970s', 'boho' are someone else's looks that you try on for a day. The appeal of these terms is that they imply a ready-made wardrobe that you can acquire with the click of a 'buy now' button. But these aesthetics are not necessarily made to last.

Within each of these aesthetics, there are a range of different Style Roots. Let's look at 'dark academia' as an example: some people love the professional, almost androgynous element of this aesthetic (Oxford baggies, layered shirts and oversized coats), whereas other people love the natural feel of this aesthetic

FIND WHAT YOU LOVE TO WEAR

(delicate patterns and frilly shirts). If you aren't in tune with your style impulses, you may end up buying into an entire aesthetic when, in fact, you only liked one part of it (ending up with lots of clothes that you don't enjoy wearing).

Despite this, I often find aesthetics a useful tool for expanding our vision of our own Style Roots. When you see that Earth, Flower and Mushroom can manifest as cottage-core, coastal grandmother, princess-core and coastal cowgirl, you realise the scope of the different ways you can experiment with fashion, while still being true to yourself and what you find exciting about style. The problem with the aesthetics-led route is you feel you want to be a cowgirl one day and a princess the next, and the binary box of 'your aesthetic' makes it seem like they are entirely separate ideas, when actually they are connected by a core root.

Take a look at the glossary on page 220 for an explanation of the aesthetics I reference in this book.

Your style is your brand

Your style can be a way to send a message about yourself into the world – and to yourself. When you wake up and go to the supermarket in jogging bottoms you hate because you're just doing an errand, what message are you sending out? Does trying to hide within an outfit make you feel good? When you go to the supermarket in the jeans with a stripey seam that makes you smile, you're telling yourself 'We're going to have fun'. Similarly, when you turn up to work wearing a grey suit because 'that's what people wear to an office' you keep your personality under wraps and don't give yourself room to shine.

Finding your Style Roots gives you the tools to communicate confidently using your clothing. Your outfit gives the person you meet a heads-up about what's coming, shows them what is special and unique about you, and lets everyone know you are someone who needs to be heard. It's a powerful tool.

02

Find what looks GOOD on *you*

Making *you shine*

Now you know what you like to wear, let's look at making that work for your body. Before you panic, I am not going to push any tired 2000s rhetoric on how to make you look smaller, taller, bigger, thinner, curvier, narrower – that was a battle we were all destined to lose. Over the years, I have discovered that there is not a single descriptor you can use for the female body that doesn't feel like an insult: short, tall, long-limbed, short-limbed, big-breasted, small-breasted, large-hipped, slim-hipped – it's ridiculous.

The idea that there is something fundamentally wrong with your body – something your clothing must hide, diminish or accentuate – is not one I am enthusiastic about. However, I don't necessarily think the answer to this is to ignore your features altogether.

Every day you dress for your body; you wear clothes that fit you, that are comfortable, that don't gape or tug in the wrong places. I believe there is a way to acknowledge your body without criticising yourself – it can actually be fun! The key is to forget what you think your body should look like, stop viewing your unique features as flaws and start afresh.

The style systems I break down in this section are all based around the idea of honouring your features. You will pinpoint your defining identifiers and echo these in your clothing. Rather than running from your bright hair, broad shoulders, small hips or long legs, you should lean in and enjoy the unique features of your body. If your body feels long and narrow, you wear clothes that are long and narrow. If you feel broad and curvy, you wear clothes

that are broad and curvy. It sounds simple, even obvious, and yet the first time I (a 1.58m/5ft 2in woman with scoliosis) realised that dressing like Kendall Jenner (a 1.78m/5ft 10in supermodel) wasn't going to make me look like Kendall Jenner, it was a shock – and a relief. The realisation that the same piece of clothing can look completely different on two different people (even if they're the same size on the tag) was a revelation. It felt completely freeing to realise: 'I can dress like me'. I discovered that I don't have to battle to change my body to match trends and I don't have to keep bullying myself in changing rooms. My body isn't wrong – the dress is wrong for

ME. My whole attitude to clothing changed – instead of grovelling to a minidress, begging it to like me and berating myself when it rejected me, I grew up and saw things in a new light. It turned out, I realised, that the dress didn't deserve me.

In this chapter I am going to break down my Body Matrix system (which will help you find the best silhouettes for your frame) and explain Colour Seasons. I will also outline some other experts' style systems that have transformed my relationship with my wardrobe, and which will help you find your best colours, fabrics, details and more.

How to find your 'types' — the L.O.N.G. method

The thing I love about the style systems ithat follow is that they aren't exactly clear-cut. Unlike traditional fruit body shapes (apple, hourglass, triangle, etc.), you can't just whip out a measuring tape and input some numbers; they are based on more complicated (but interesting) sets of rules. My method for distilling systems and applying them to your features goes as follows. Come back and review this page with fresh eyes once you have reached the end of this chapter.

Step 1: *LEARN the nuances and differences between the different types*

I have made my explanations as clear as possible to help you understand what is unique about each of the Body Matrix types (page 120) and Colour Seasons (page 141). You can use my lists or research systems on the internet to really understand them inside and out. These systems aren't simple, so they require some learning to get to grips with. Understanding the basic rules for what makes a body one type or another is essential for finding yourself within them.

Step 2: Get *OBJECTIVE*

To settle on a 'type' within each system, you first have to look at your body in some depth. Defining whether your face is long or short, your shoulders round or pointed, your eye aqua-blue or slate-grey is a necessary component. You can do this in a couple of ways.

Line drawings: For body and face types, you can try drawing an outline of your face or body to help you become objective about the shapes you see. I go into this in more depth on page 106.

Getting an outside opinion: One of the simplest ways to get objective is to ask for the opinions of others. You could ask friends, family or groups like Reddit or Facebook. You don't have to directly ask their opinion on your type, although you can, but rather how they would describe you or your features: Does my face seem long to you? Do my eyes seem soft? Is my waist straight? You might get a lot of 'your hips are fine' or 'you are beautiful the way you are' so feel free to explain to them that this isn't an exercise in changing yourself but understanding who you are.

With that said, be sure to ask people you trust, or participate in forums with a kind culture and strict guidelines.

So many women I know are completely wrong about their features; some see big hips where there is none, a straight waist when they've got a rounded one, a big or small chest when they are moderate. Our perceptions of ourselves are disrupted by what society tells us we are supposed to look like so it's hard to see how we truly appear.

Step 3: **NARROW-DOWN**

Now you have defined your features, you can 'play snap' with the Body Matrix types or Colour Seasons. The goal is to find the types with which you have the most in common. You may have things in common with multiple types, which is where the systems get a little tricky. Use my descriptions to help you discover which ones you can't be. You could use a key feature like 'squarish shoulders' or 'brown eyes' to eliminate multiple types at once.

Note: *you are unlikely to have every feature of every type, for example you might have short arms rather than long but everything else matches.*

Step 4: *Trust your GUT*

At the end of the day, you have to make a call. Many of these systems are not simple or clean-cut, so there are likely to be multiple options that sort-of fit you. At this stage in the process, once you have narrowed-down the options based on the rules, and you know how to define your features, you must follow your gut on which option best fits you.

Take each of these steps out of context and they don't work; without knowing the differences between the types and knowing the rules inside and out, making a call based on your gut instinct will probably take you in the wrong direction. Similarly, if you cannot trust your gut to make a final decision, you will never settle as the rules don't always lead in one clear direction. Without getting objective about your features and defining each one, it will be unclear how the rules apply to you, and you will not be able to make an informed call.

FIND WHAT LOOKS GOOD ON YOU

The Body Matrix

Why we should talk about our bodies

There is a widely held belief that it is inherently anti-feminist, self-derogatory and self-loathing to apply descriptors to our bodies, even more so to imply that what you should wear should be affected by these descriptors. When I first discovered body-type dressing, I was completely fascinated, but also wary. Can you still talk about women's bodies like this? Isn't that wrong?

The fact that body-type dressing has been used as a part of body-type bullying doesn't mean acknowledging your features through your clothing is inherently nasty. You can describe your body without listing the things you hate about it or viewing those descriptors as negatives to be changed and hidden. Describing your body in neutral-positive terms frees so many women from the idea that their body should look a certain

way. It's the realisation that there are dozens of women out there with similar body features; there are celebrities who are upheld for their beauty for the very thing you hate about yourself; that you use your body as a superpower to wear clothes other people struggle to wear; and that not every trend is made for you.

Before you panic, the system that I am about to introduce to you is not about 'balancing your features' or morphing your body to look like an hourglass. There is no perfect body type that you are trying to masquerade as – you are simply going to learn what feels most harmonious with your shape. You might feel an initial negative response to certain words I encourage you to use, such as 'wide' or 'round'. We are going to view these terms as neutral and use them with love rather than criticism.

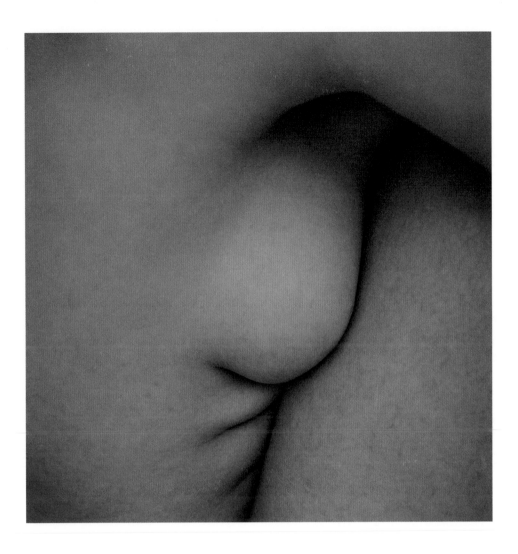

Please note that none of the key words used in this chapter are referring to fat; roundness is not fat, wideness is not fat, softness is not fat. The same applies to being thin or skinny: narrowness is not thinness; straightness is not thinness. You can have any of the Body Lines at any weight, but your lines may change depending on how your body gains or loses weight.

Why are body systems so complicated?

While studying existing style systems that focus on body, face and colour, I realised something: they are SO unnecessarily complicated. Don't get me wrong, as a literature graduate, I enjoy exploring the nuances of systems of intellectually minded people, and it's enjoyable to see their enthusiasm leaping off the page. However, when it comes to our bodies, sometimes the complications can keep us on the hamster wheel of trying to figure out our 'type' without ever finding what really works for us. Having spent a lot of time learning these systems, putting them into practice for thousands of people, and sometimes failing, I realised that there were certain things I would personally prioritise, that these existing systems currently do not. I believe that dressing in a way that makes you come alive, feel comfortable and confident, doesn't have to be so hard.

Discovering your Body Matrix

We have all seen body types go in and out of fashion: hourglass in the 1950s, petite in the 1960s, athletic in the 1980s, skinny in the 1990s, curvy in the 2010s – it is impossible to keep up. I don't believe we should treat our bodies like trends but instead should recognise the timelessly beautiful aspects of our own individual figures. There is something unique and exciting about your build that can be emphasised with clothing. Rather than forcing your body to fit a mould, you should effortlessly embrace the contours of your frame.

I have identified three key elements that play a role in any outfit's silhouette: width, length and shape. I call these the Body Lines – these are at the foundation of so many styling and body-typing systems. You can look at the shape and lines of your body to indicate how to incorporate each of these into your outfits. Each of us falls somewhere on the three dichotomies: wide vs narrow, short vs long, straight vs round.

WIDTH	wide	medium	narrow
LENGTH	short	medium	long
SHAPE	round	medium	straight

For example, I could be considered narrow, short and round. I would think of my mum as wide, medium, and straight. To define where you sit, you simply identify which features are the most dominant in your frame. Try the exercise on page 108 to work out where each element of your body falls within the three groups. Your shoulders, chest and hips play the most important role, but you should also pay attention to your limbs, hands and feet. When trying to define your features, you are looking at the overall picture of your body, rather than focusing on one or two details. I don't find measurements particularly helpful here – you have to learn to be intuitive and get comfortable being in the presence of your own body.

The idea is that you then echo the shapes and lines of your body with your clothing. Width is mirrored in your necklines, sleeves, cuffs, hems, and accessories. Length is reflected in the length and size of your outfit. Shape is adapted through silhouette, patterns and fabrics.

Width: Necklines, sleeves, cuffs, hems, and accessories.

Length: Length, size.

Shape: Silhouette, shape, patterns, fabric.

What about weight change?

I really detest the stereotypical recommendations for weight gain. So many magazines and stylists treat 'plus-size' as a body type category, as if everyone over a certain weight looks good in the same clothes. This notion is as ridiculous as saying any two people who are slim look good in the same things. I mention this because it's a question I get asked frequently: 'But what if I gain weight? Won't the things I look good in change?'

There are so many stereotypes about gaining weight that I have seen women's bodies prove untrue again and again. Some people feel they look more round as they gain weight, some people feel they look larger, some people feel broader and some feel they look shorter. In my experience of looking at women's bodies, gaining weight usually emphasises the features we already have. A change in weight, whether gaining or losing, can feel like a shock and can take an adjustment period. However, rather than jumping into wearing oversized, loose-fitting clothes like the magazines tell you to, take a moment to think about the new shapes that you see in the mirror. What if, instead of dressing for 'fat' or 'skinny', we dress for our shape and Body Lines? Some plus-sized women look incredible in flowing tops and wide-leg trousers, whereas on some, figure-hugging, curve-enhancing silhouettes show off their beauty. This is true for women of all shapes and sizes – what looks good on one person, won't necessarily look good on another.

A silhouette system

Some body-type systems combine vibe or aesthetic with silhouette. While I think this is a fun way of looking at your figure, I am not sure that it is always the most helpful place to start, as you can get caught up in the style rather than the fit. None of the Body Lines I am going to explain here is associated with a certain style (although you can combine your silhouette keywords with your Style Roots – see page 22). Sticking to a silhouette system is the most effective way of expressing your style and finding clothes that make you shine.

The Body Lines

Your Body Lines are the silhouettes that best echo the shapes of your body. Your lines can refer to the lines of your limbs, chest, hips and so on, but can also mean the clothing you wear. For example, most midi skirts have a straight line, a peplum dress has round lines, a maxi dress has long lines. Your best lines are the ones that reflect your own features.

There are 27 unique combinations of Body Lines, for example:

○ **wide** + **short** + **round**

○ **medium** + **long** + **straight**

It goes without saying that there are more than 27 different women's body shapes in the world, but the point of dressing for your body is to lean into your dominant features rather than the pernickety ones that differ for every woman.

As much as I would love to break down the best lines for each of the 27 combinations, this book would go on forever! However, I thought I would visually show you the principles behind the system using the eight 'extreme' combinations and one medium example – find them littered throughout this section.

How do you know if you have narrow or wide shoulders? Rather than comparing your shoulders to your hips and determining which one is widest (as you might in other systems), look at the point where your shoulder meets/becomes your arm. If this point extends significantly outwards from the upper point of your armpit, this is a good indication of wide shoulders. If this point is directly above or close to the upper point of your armpit, this is a sign of narrowness in your shoulders.

Width: narrow vs wide

The width in your frame refers to how narrow or wide your body feels. Make sure to pay attention to more than just your shoulders or your hips. Think about the overall picture of your bone structure and whether it is blunt and wide, or narrow and thin.

A note on pear shapes: *When it comes to 'pear shapes', you are more likely to be narrow than wide, even though you have wide hips. Narrowness in the shoulders often means narrowness in the limbs, upper chest, hands and feet too, which cancels out the width in the hips and means your line is more narrow than anything else.*

Reversely, being slim-hipped can be a sign of narrowness, but if you also have wide shoulders, it is more likely that wide lines would be a better fit for you.

If you have wide shoulders *and* wide hips, but narrowness in the upper body or waist, you are more likely to suit wide shapes than narrow ones.

NARROW

You might be narrow if you have narrow, sloped shoulders, slim hips or delicate-feeling bones. Narrowness is complemented by narrow shapes in clothing, such as cinched sleeves or cuffs. Narrow lines come inward, rather than outward, and have a closed, rather than open, feel.

Key words

- Cinched
- Closed
- Gathered
- Narrow
- Nipped
- Pinched

Best lines

Closed necklines:
- Collars
- Crew neck
- Halter neck
- High boatneck
- Mock neck
- Turtleneck

Cinched cuffs:
- Batwing sleeve
- Bishop sleeve
- Harem pants
- Paperbag trousers

wide + short + round

wide round sleeve

high waist

wide round bag

chunky round sandals

wide leg

Narrow shapes:
- Skinny jeans
- Cigarette pants
- Fitted sleeve

Narrow hemline:
- Pencil skirt
- Fishtail/mermaid skirt
- Tulip skirt
- Straight skirt

Nipped waist

Narrow straps:
- If you were wearing a camisole, the straps would be placed towards the neck rather than the shoulders/armpits.

Narrow shoes:
- Stilettos
- Pointed toes
- Sock boots
- Tight knee boots
- Narrow flats

Narrow accessories:
- Thin bangle
- Thin ring band
- Drop earrings
- Light, narrow chain necklace/bracelet
- Thin headband

WIDE

You might be wide if you have wide or broad shoulders, blunt/wide limb bones that have an athletic or robust feel, wide hips, or wide hands and feet. Width is complemented by wide shapes in clothing, such as wide necklines, open sleeves, or flared legs. Wide lines go outward rather than inward and have an open rather than closed feel.

Key words

- Flared
- Flowing
- Free
- Loose
- Open
- Wide

Best lines

Open necklines:
- Off the shoulder
- Low boatneck
- Wide V-neck
- Square neckline
- Bardot neckline
- Round neck

Wide sleeves:
- Bell sleeve
- Flutter sleeve
- Flounce sleeve
- Kimono sleeve

Wide shoulder seams

Wide strap placement

Flared legs:
- ○ Bell bottoms
- ○ Bootcut
- ○ Palazzo pants
- ○ Sailor pants
- ○ Wide leg

Flared skirts:
- ○ A-line skirt
- ○ Full skirt
- ○ Skater skirt
- ○ Wrap skirt

Heavy shoes:
- ○ Wedges
- ○ Chunky boots
- ○ Chunky loafer

Chunky accessories:
- ○ Wide bangle
- ○ Wide hoop earrings
- ○ Heavy chain necklace/ bracelet
- ○ Thick ring band
- ○ Beaded necklace
- ○ Wide headband

Length: long vs short

When it comes to long and short lines, there are so many interesting ideas within body-type communities. I love the concept of the long/short vertical line that is frequently used within David Kibbe's image IDs (more on this on page 167): if you have a long vertical line, it means you look taller than you really are, and if you have a short vertical line, you look shorter than you really are. When considering whether you are long or short in the Body Matrix, think about your vertical line (your perceived height) considered in partnership with your real height. For example, even if you are 180cm/5ft 11in, you might be perceived as looking slightly shorter than that, although slightly shorter than 180cm/5ft 11in is still quite tall, so 'long' would probably still be the best option for you.

Here is a general guide:

1.6m/5ft 3in and below: You are likely short and look best in short lines.

1.6–1.7m/5ft 4in–5ft 7in: You are likely a medium height and look best in medium lines.

1.7m/5ft 8in and above: You are likely tall and look best in long lines.

wide + long + round

large round hat

wide neckline

waist definition

long skirt

waist definition

large round bag

long coat

high round wide shoe

wide + long + straight

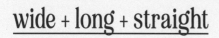

open neckline

heavy fabric

long draped coat

long straight bag

straight trouser

chunky sandals

LONG

You might be long if you have a long vertical line, are above 1.7m/5ft 7in, have long limbs, a long chest or upper body and long hands, feet or fingers. Length is complemented by long clothing. This means longer than standard: for example, a midi skirt or coat would be best below rather than above the knee; a pair of trousers would be best below the ankle; and the hem of a top or jacket would be best below, rather than above, the hip bone. Conversely, people with a long vertical line can also look stunning in items with extremely short lines, such as a mini skirt, as this enhances their length – in this case their long legs. Someone with long lines will also be complemented by large shapes and patterns.

Key words

- Large
- Long

Best lines

Maxi lengths:

- Maxi skirt
- Maxi dress

Unbroken lines:

- **Note:** *this is where the colour, pattern or silhouette runs from top to bottom and is not broken into sections.*

Long sleeves

High heels

Long toes of shoes

Knee-length or thigh-high boots

Large accessories

Long accessories:

- Long handbags
- Long cross body bags
- Long necklace

Oval or rectangle shapes as opposed to circle or square shapes

Large patterns:

- **Note:** *A general rule for floral or round patterns: if it's bigger than your palm, it's probably too big for you!*
- Vertical-leaning patterns such as vertical stripes

High skirt slits

Extremely high or low waist

SHORT

You might be short if you have a short vertical line, are below 1.6m/5ft 4in, have short limbs, a short chest or upper body, and short hands, feet or fingers. A short length is complemented by short clothing. This means shorter than standard: for example, a midi skirt or coat would be best above rather than below the knee; a pair of trousers or maxi skirt would be best above the ankle; and the hem of a top or jacket would be best above, rather than below, the hip bone. Someone with short lines will be complemented by small shapes and patterns.

Key words

- Little
- Short
- Small

Best lines

Mini lengths:
- Mini skirt
- Mini dress
- Cropped top
- Cropped jacket
- Cropped jeans

Broken lines:
- **Note:** *this is when the colour, pattern, or silhouette is broken up into sections rather than flowing from top to bottom of the outfit.*

Short sleeves

Delicate shoes:
- Kitten heels
- Ballet flats

Short toes

Small/miniature patterns

Small accessories

Short accessories:
- Short handbags
- Short necklaces

Circle or square shapes as opposed to rectangular or oval shapes

narrow + short + round

narrow straps

open neckline

waist definition

soft draped fabric

round narrow bag

narrow toe

cinched leg

wide + short + straight

wide floaty top

straight shape

wide short jacket

wide cropped leg

chunky sandals

short wide bag

Shape: round vs straight

It is in this category that you are most likely to think of the extremes: Audrey Hepburn and Marilyn Monroe. Often with shape, people immediately categorise themselves as medium because they don't think of themselves as fitting into the perceived extremes of 'round' and 'straight'. I urge you to wait before you do! Especially if you are slender, you are unlikely to think of yourself as 'curvy' when in fact you may well have soft round shapes in your frame that will be honoured by soft shapes in an outfit. You do not have to be typically voluptuous to need round shapes, nor have a pencil-like frame to suit straight shapes. Be sure to consider your shoulders, chest and hips when deciding on shape – these are the most important factors.

ROUND

You might be round if you have round shapes throughout your frame: round shoulders (especially shoulder points where the shoulder meets the arm), a round chest, round hips, a defined waist, and a round shape to your arms and legs. Round types will feel soft: even when

> When talking about roundness, I am not referring to a round tummy or an apple shape. A round tummy is less significant to your silhouette than you might imagine — you can have a round tummy whether you have a curvy shape in your frame or a straight shape to your frame.

they are thin or slender, they will have a soft fleshy feel. Those with a significant round shape in the chest, but more of a straight shape in the hips, are likely to need round shapes in their silhouettes. Round types look best when they wear round, soft and circular silhouettes. They will look best in shapes that define the waist and accommodate the round shapes in their chest and hips.

Key words

- o   Circular
- o   Curvy
- o   Fitted
- o   Hourglass
- o   Open
- o   Round
- o   Soft

Best lines

High waist:
- High waists help define the waist – the waist of the garment should hit your natural waist point.

Fitted waist:
- A blazer with a clear waist indentation
- Belted waist
- Wrap tops and dresses

Round, open necklines:
- Scoop neck
- Sweetheart neckline
- Round strapless neckline
- Queen Anne neckline
- Rounded v-neck

Bootleg trouser shape:
- Flattering for round shapes as it continues the hourglass shape down the leg.

Tight trousers:
- Cigarette pants
- Skinny jeans

Round skirt shapes:
- Pencil skirt
- Peplum skirt

Round hems and collars

Ruffles

Ruching

Clingy fabrics:
- A turtleneck is a closed neckline but shows off the round shapes of the chest and waist.

Round patterns:
- Florals
- Polka dots
- Waves
- Circles
- Love hearts
- Round lace

Round accessories:
- Round pendants
- Round stones in rings
- Round handbags
- Pearl jewellery

Round-toed shoes

Round sleeves:
- Puff sleeves
- Batwing sleeve
- Bishop sleeve
- Bell sleeve

Soft sleeves:
- Flutter sleeves

Soft fabrics:
- Velvet
- Chiffon

narrow + long + round

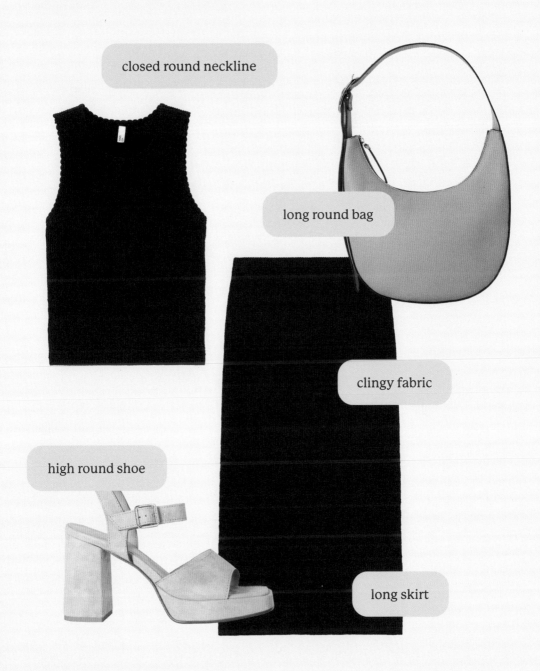

closed round neckline

long round bag

clingy fabric

high round shoe

long skirt

STRAIGHT

You might be straight if you have straight shapes throughout your frame: straight, flat shoulders, pointed shoulders, straight chest and hips, straight waist, or a straight look to the arms and legs. No matter the weight of someone who has straight lines, their flesh will look taut rather than soft. Straight types look best when they honour their straightness with geometric and stiff lines.

Key words

○ Angular
○ Geometric
○ Sharp
○ Stiff
○ Straight
○ Structured

Best lines

Pointed collars

Straight waist:
○ Avoid fitted or defined waists

Straight trouser shapes:
○ Straight leg
○ Cigarette pants

Geometric patterns:
○ Chevron
○ Stripes
○ Plaid/check
○ Gingham
○ Houndstooth
○ Argyle
○ Diamond

Straight, closed necklines:
○ Grandad collar
○ Crew neck
○ Boat neck
○ Square neckline
○ Straight strapless neckline
○ Bardot neckline

Stiff, structured fabric
○ Poplin
○ Stiff cotton

Straight skirt shapes:
○ Straight skirt
○ Column skirt
○ Some pencil skirts
○ Bias cut

Straight sleeves and hems

Angular shapes:
○ Rectangle
○ Square
○ Hexagon

Straight accessories:
○ Angular handbag
○ Geometric pendant
○ Long straight necklace
○ Angular ring

Pointed shoes

narrow + short + straight

short straight bag

narrow waistcoat

straight
structured shorts

pointed narrow shoe

narrow + long + straight

long straight dress

long
structured bag

sharp shoe

structured shirt

medium + medium + medium

single-breasted
soft-fabric blazer

simple camisole

mid-waist jeans

moderate-sized bag

slightly rounded trainers

FIND WHAT LOOKS GOOD ON YOU

Medium

For any of the previous dichotomies, you might think yourself in the 'medium' category. Before you jump to medium, however, which is the most tempting option, let me reframe this for you: almost nobody is truly medium. Almost everybody leans round or straight. Rather than looking for the extremes of wide/ narrow, look to see which way you lean. The little leans we have offer big clues as to which lines will best suit us. If you truly do not lean either way, go for medium. You might have medium width if you have shoulders that are neither particularly wide nor narrow, a frame that feels moderately in between wide and narrow. If you have medium in your frame, you will best suit moderate, simple, even versions of any silhouette. You might use the word 'slightly' to describe various clothing features.

Key words

- Balanced
- Clean
- Even
- Medium
- Moderate
- Neat
- Neutral
- Proportionate
- Simple

Best lines – medium width

Even necklines (these are the simplest necklines – not particularly wide or closed, they will sit somewhere in the middle):

- Crew neck
- Square neck
- Simple V-neck
- Grandad collar

Medium sleeves

Accessories with moderate thickness

Minimal layers

Best lines – medium length

Three-quarter length sleeves

Midi lengths:

- Midi skirt
- Midi dress
- Ankle-length trousers
- Hip-length jacket

Moderate-sized patterns

Moderate-sized accessories

Clean lines

Best lines – medium shape

Medium patterns:
- Waves
- Paisley

Plain fabrics

Clean cut:
- Clean, straight hems
- Clean shapes

Simple shapes:
- Stripes
- Polka dots

Find your Body Lines

Hopefully, having read through these descriptions, you should have a strong idea of which way you lean for each of the three dichotomies (width, length, shape). The key is to look at the overall impression of your figure, which might feel like quite an overwhelming task if you are not used to thinking about your body in this way! You might fixate on a specific feature and find yourself unable to see the big picture or look at your body and be unable to see anything other than: 'this is me'. The key is to be more objective.

To view your frame objectively, it's useful to try the line drawing exercise. This helps take YOU out of the picture and also helps you to view your body in shapes rather than body parts.

1. Take a picture of yourself (make sure the camera is facing you straight on at chest height).

2. Print the photo and grab some tracing paper OR import the photo into a program like Procreate OR use the marker tool in your phone's photo app.

medium, short, round

- Round shoulders
- Short round limbs
- Defined waist
- Round chest and hips

narrow, long, straight

- Narrow shoulders
- Long straight limbs
- Straight chest and hips

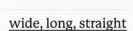

wide, long, straight

- Wide shoulders
- Long limbs
- Straight chest

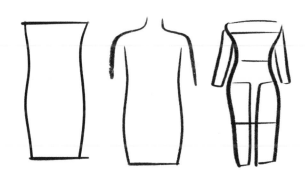

wide, short, round

- Wide shoulders
- Round chest and hips
- Short limbs
- Short vertical line

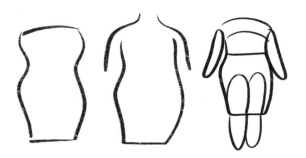

	width	length	shape
shoulders			
arms			
chest/bust			
hips			
legs			
OVERALL			

EXAMPLE	width	length	shape
shoulders	narrow	short	round
arms	narrow	medium	straight
chest/bust	narrow	short	round
hips	medium	medium	round
legs	narrow	medium	medium
OVERALL	narrow	short	round

3. Trace the shapes in your body as abstract shapes. I like to do a few different kinds of drawing to get different perspectives.

4. Now use this collection of shapes to fill out the table overleaf. It's not a test – there aren't necessarily any right answers! Note down what seems right to you based on what you can see in the lines you've drawn. Remember to be kind and honest with yourself.

Example:

From my list you can see I am majority narrow, short and round. Even though I have a couple of medium features, overall I lean short and round.

If you still feel stuck between the dichotomies, it can help to do a little brainstorming using other descriptors. Take a piece of paper and pen and write down the shapes you see. You can brainstorm for your overall figure, or individual features like shoulders. For example, you might try to name the shape of your hips: circular, square, hexagonal? Key word prompts:

WIDTH
- Angular
- Broad
- Delicate
- Heavy
- Large
- Light
- Moderate
- Petite
- Robust
- Small
- Trim
- Wispy

LENGTH
- Compact
- Large
- Small

SHAPE
- Boxy
- Circular
- Curved
- Diamond
- Fleshy
- Oval
- Pointed
- Rectangular
- Sharp
- Sloped
- Soft
- Squarish
- Taut

Combining your Body Lines

When combining your lines, you should consider fusing them in each piece as well as your overall outfit. In other words, let's say you were wide, you might find a top that has an open neckline and wide sleeves, in which case, great! However, if you have a top that you love that has a closed neckline and narrow sleeves, you need to add the width elsewhere in the outfit (for example, pairing the top with a flared trouser or flowing skirt).

You might find that some of your lines contradict each other, in which case, you need to experiment with how you can fuse them in your personal style choices. For example, if you are narrow and rounded, for the former you want closed necklines, and the latter open ones. To find a solution to this, you need to work out necklines that fuse both of these elements – like a halter neck (which is open at the bust but closed at the neck) or a Queen Anne neckline (which is somewhat like a halter neck but with filled out sleeves). Similarly, you might opt for a closed neckline but ensure your outfit has waist definition.

When looking at the recommendations for your lines, you might find that you don't like some of your options. If you don't feel comfortable in a high neck, who am I to tell you otherwise? I suggest you use the necklines, sleeves and waist heights as a guide, not a set of rules you must always follow. From the lists I have suggested for your features, feel free to pick and choose based on your taste, personal style and experience. However, with that said, I encourage you to move out of your comfort zone and try things you may not have experimented with before or worn in a long time – you might see them in a new light! For example, I used to hate harem pants because people kept pairing them with blazers (which I felt looked silly), however, experimenting with them in a summery beach context, I found they complemented my figure and so I have embraced a few pairs in my wardrobe.

Your best colours

Colour is the easiest element of your wardrobe to upgrade. It is one of the first things we visually process, so it is the simplest way to tell a story about yourself and enable you to look your best. It is the most effective 'lift' in your wardrobe – when you wear your best colours, you will look brighter and more exciting.

There is a lot of fiction surrounding the use of colour that on first inspection sounds plausible, but which limits your potential to shine. Most of these centre on the colour black: 'black suits everyone', 'black is slimming', 'black hides the dirt'. These handy catchphrases make it sound like wearing black is foolproof, when in fact black is harsh and looks messy on a lot of people.

Neutrals are the foundation of many people's wardrobes, but you probably own the wrong ones (most people find themselves drawn to versions of beige, navy, burgundy, khaki, black and white). As someone who used to have a wardrobe full of tan, black and white, I understand how easy it can be to head in the wrong direction. Most of us have no idea about the range of neutral tones out there or how they interact with and complement other colours.

Unlike many anti-classic stylists out there, I don't think that splashing yourself with a rainbow instantly makes your style good, or even interesting. However, I do think most of us are not making use of the range of colours out there to bring life and interest to our outfits. Personally, I am tired of seeing the same classic, neutral outfit on my social media feed again and again. When you dress within your Colour Season, you find colours you would have never dared to try or imagined you could wear.

The concept of Colour Seasons was largely developed by Kathryn Kalisz, often referred to as the sci\ art system. The advice I outline in this section is an amalgamation of Kalisz's theory, research from various corners of the internet, feedback from my clients and followers, and my own experience.

The four Colour Season elements

The Colour Seasons are based on four elements.

Cool vs Warm

Cool colours are closer to blue, whereas warm colours are closer to yellow. For example, a cool green would be a blue-green, whereas a warm green would be a yellow-green. A cool pink would be a purple-pink, whereas a warm pink would be a peachy pink. A cool brown would be chocolatey, olive or mushroom brown, whereas a warm brown would be a rusty, copper or fiery brown. You can lean 'neutral', which means between warm and cool, but almost everyone leans slightly one way or another.

Light vs Dark

Light colours are closer to white, whereas dark colours are closer to black. You can be medium.

Soft vs Bright

Bright colours are 'clear' which means they are the purest version of their colour. Soft colours are infused with grey or brown, so they have a dullness or muddiness to them. You can be 'medium', so somewhere between soft and bright.

Contrast

Contrast ranges from high to low. If you have very dark hair and very light skin and eyes, you have high contrast, whereas if your hair colour is the same darkness as your skin and eyes you are considered low contrast. You can be somewhere in the middle between high and low contrast.

Low contrast:

High contrast:

The idea is that you echo your features in your clothing so that you are wearing the colour rather than the colour wearing you. If the colours in your face are soft, the colours you wear should be soft. When you echo your features, you allow your features to shine.

Find the colours in your face here:

o **Hair:** Eyelashes, eyebrows, head hair.

o **Eyes:** All colours found in and around (at the edge of) your iris.

o **Skin:** Cheeks, forehead, and lips.

There are various methods to help pin down your Colour Seasons. A popular one is the 'draping method', which is when you place clothing of different tones under your chin and see how the light reflects against your features (do look this up online as it's very interesting). My method involves defining your features and matching them with the corresponding Colour Seasons that echoes you.

Finding Your Colour Seasons

This quiz should help you settle on a Colour Season. This can help with steps two and three (get objective + narrow down) of the L.O.N.G. Method (page 98). Remember to assess your natural features, without makeup, in bright daylight (preferably by a window).

Circle the answers that best represent what you see.

PHASE 1: *Defining your features*

I would describe my eyes as ... (you can select more than one)

○ green-blue	○ turquoise	○ reddish brown
○ icy blue	○ apple green	○ amber
○ grey blue	○ green hazel	○ ochre
○ sky blue	○ honey	○ mustard
○ indigo	○ almond	○ dark grey
○ ash grey	○ chestnut brown	○ jet black
○ mushroom grey	○ chocolate brown	○ other _____

These colours/this colour feels ...

○ warm/cool?	○ light/dark?	○ soft/bright?
○ warm	○ light	○ soft
○ slightly warm	○ slightly light	○ slightly soft
○ neutral	○ medium	○ medium
○ slightly cool	○ slightly dark	○ slightly bright
○ cool	○ dark	○ bright

I would describe my hair colour (hair, eyebrows, eyelashes) as …
(you can select more than one)

- icy white
- creamy white
- ashy blonde
- mousy blonde
- dark blonde
- dirty blonde
- yellow blonde
- strawberry blonde
- honey blonde
- reddish mousy

- light ashy brown
- mousy brown
- golden brown
- caramel brown
- espresso brown
- bronde
- copper red
- ginger
- fiery orange
- rich reddish brown

- dark ashy brown
- chocolate brown
- ink black
- blue-black
- silver grey
- grey-white
- salt and pepper
- mushroom grey
- warm grey
- other _____

These colours/this colour feels …

- warm/cool?
  - warm
  - slightly warm
  - neutral
  - slightly cool
  - cool

- light/dark?
  - light
  - slightly light
  - medium
  - slightly dark
  - dark

- soft/bright?
  - soft
  - slightly soft
  - medium
  - slightly bright
  - bright

My forehead/cheek skin is ... (you can select more than one)

- icy white
- translucent pink
- translucent peach
- ivory
- porcelain
- cream
- pale pink
- pinky grey
- purpley grey
- pale peach

- honey
- mushroom
- beige
- almond
- caramel
- sand
- golden beige
- amber
- warm brown
- reddish brown

- coffee brown
- chestnut brown
- chocolate brown
- deep golden brown
- deep ashy brown
- deep brown
- blue-black
- other _____

These colours/this colour feels ...

- warm/cool?
  - warm
  - slightly warm
  - neutral
  - slightly cool
  - cool

- light/dark?
  - light
  - slightly light
  - medium
  - slightly dark
  - dark

- soft/bright?
  - soft
  - slightly soft
  - medium
  - slightly bright
  - bright

My lip skin is ... (you can select more than one)

- pinky nude
- peachy nude
- nude brown
- pale pink
- soft pink
- icy pink
- icy purple

- rosy pink
- fuchsia pink
- beige
- terracotta
- soft red
- cherry red
- deep red

- cinnamon brown
- deep brown
- mauve
- purple brown
- other _____

These colours/this colour feels ...

- ○ warm/cool?
    - ○ warm
    - ○ slightly warm
    - ○ neutral
    - ○ slightly cool
    - ○ cool
- ○ light/dark?
    - ○ light
    - ○ slightly light
    - ○ medium
    - ○ slightly dark
    - ○ dark
- ○ soft/bright?
    - ○ soft
    - ○ slightly soft
    - ○ medium
    - ○ slightly bright
    - ○ bright

My contrast is ...

- ○ low
- ○ slightly low
- ○ medium
- ○ slightly high
- ○ high

RESULTS

Count the number of answers that were warm and those that were cool —
whichever you have the most of tick the box below.

Repeat for light vs dark, then soft vs bright.

- ○ warm/cool
    - ○ warm
    - ○ cool
- ○ light/dark?
    - ○ light
    - ○ dark
- ○ soft/bright?
    - ○ soft
    - ○ bright

PHASE 2: Order your features

You know now if you are generally warm/cool, light/dark, soft/bright. Now
you need to find which of these three categories is most dominant in your
features. You can do this by counting how many times each category came
up for you in the quiz. The most common category is dominant and sits in
position no.1, the second most common sits in position no.2, and the third
most common sits in position no.3. For example: 1. light 2. cool 3. bright

PHASE 3: *Match with the 12 Colour Seasons*

Highlight the season below that most closely matches your top three features and their order of dominance.

- Dark Winter: dark, cool, soft (for a winter)
- True Winter: cool, medium-dark, medium-bright
- Bright Winter: bright, cool, light (for a winter)
- Bright Spring: bright, warm, dark (for a spring)
- True Spring: warm, medium-bright, medium-light
- Light Spring: light, warm, soft (for a spring)
- Light Summer: light, cool, bright (for a summer)
- True Summer: cool, medium-soft, medium-light
- Soft Summer: soft, cool, dark (for a summer)
- Soft Autumn: soft, warm, light (for an autumn)
- True Autumn: warm, medium-soft, medium-dark
- Dark Autumn: dark, warm, bright (for an autumn)

Whenever I say 'for a winter/spring/summer/autumn' this means that in the context of that season, this particular element is a defining feature. For example, I specify that Dark Winter (page 142) is 'soft (for a Winter)'. This means that, in the context of the Winter season, softness will be a defining feature for that person. But in the context of the 12 Colour Seasons, they are not that soft.

The 12 Colour Seasons

If you've completed the quiz, you should now have a rough idea of your Colour Season. Use the following pages to confirm your decision and discover your best colours.

Winters

The winter category is defined by bright, cool and dark features.

Springs

The spring category is defined by warm, bright and light features.

Summers

The summer category is defined by cool, soft and light features.

Autumns

The autumn category is defined by warm, dark and soft features.

Dark Winter

This is the darkest and softest category of the winters. They are defined by their dark and deep features.

Ranking

1. Dark
2. Cool
3. Soft (for a winter)

Contrast

Medium

Key words

- Berry
- Cool
- Deep
- Jewel
- Rich
- Smoky
- Stormy

Signature colour

Purple

Typical features

Hair

- Black
- Deep brown
- Soft-medium brown

Eyes

- Olive green
- Olive brown
- Cool hazel
- Deep brown
- Deep black

Skin

- Off white
- Cool beige
- Chocolate brown
- Blue-black

Lips

- Berry red
- Cool brown
- Purpley nude
- Burgundy

Blues

- O Deep blue
- O Soft navy
- O Navy grey
- O Cyan blue

Greens

- O Deep jade green
- O Dark turquoise

Yellows

- O Deep banana yellow

Oranges

- O Burnt peach
- O Dark coral

Reds

- O Wine

Pinks

- O Soft deep pink
- O Deep berry pink
- O Pink terracotta
- O Cranberry
- O Deep rose

Purples

- O Grape
- O Maroon

True Winter

This is the coolest category of the winters. They are defined by their icy colouring, and only slightly dark and bright-leaning features.

Ranking

1. Cool
2. Medium-dark
3. Medium-bright

Contrast

Medium-high

Key words

○ Berry
○ Clear
○ Cool
○ Frosty
○ Icy
○ Smoky

Signature colour

Pink

Typical features

Hair

○ Soft black
○ Deep brown
○ Dark mousy brown
○ Medium ashy brown

Eyes

○ Medium chocolate brown
○ Light mushroom brown
○ Slate grey
○ Deep blue
○ Navy blue
○ Deep blue-grey
○ Icy blue
○ Emerald green

Skin

○ Pinky nude
○ Off white
○ Cool beige
○ Mushroom brown
○ Chocolate brown

Lips

○ Berry red
○ Cool brown
○ Ballet pink
○ Purple nude

Some colours in the *True Winter palette*

Blues

- ○ Royal blue
- ○ Pale cerulean
- ○ Sky blue
- ○ Denim

Greens

- ○ Deep mint
- ○ Light sea green
- ○ Icy, pastel green
- ○ Teal

Yellows

- ○ Banana

Reds

- ○ Deep rose
- ○ Cranberry

Pinks

- ○ Raspberry pink
- ○ Light rose
- ○ Pastel pink
- ○ Magenta
- ○ Fuchsia pink

Purples

- ○ Amethyst
- ○ Lavender
- ○ Iris

Bright Winter

This is the brightest and lightest type of the winters. They will have very dark features including dark hair, eyes or skin combined with light skin or eyes.

Ranking

1. Bright
2. Cool
3. Light (for a winter)

Contrast

High

Key words

- Bright
- Candyfloss
- Christmassy
- Electric
- Frosty
- Icy
- Neon
- Pastel

Signature colour

Red

Typical features

Hair

- Jet black
- Blue-black
- Deep chocolate brown

Eyes

- Coal black
- Deep chocolate brown
- Icy blue
- Sky blue
- Blue-grey
- Icy grey
- Electric blue
- Turquoise green
- Emerald green

Skin

- Porcelain
- Icy white
- Pinky nude
- Chocolate brown
- Blue-black

Lips

- Cherry red
- Fuchsia pink
- Ballet pink
- Pinky nude

Some colours in the Bright Winter palette

Blues

- ○ Blueberry
- ○ Ocean
- ○ Crystal blue

Greens

- ○ Jade
- ○ Aqua green

Yellows

- ○ Banana yellow
- ○ Lemon yellow

Oranges

- ○ Neon orange

Reds

- ○ Carmine
- ○ Rose red

Pinks

- ○ Fuchsia
- ○ Hot pink
- ○ Raspberry

Purples

- ○ Royal purple

Bright Spring

This is the brightest and darkest of the springs. They can have dark hair and eyes, combined with light skin and/or eyes, and have a golden glow.

Ranking

1. Bright
2. Warm
3. Dark (for a spring)

Contrast

High

Key words

○ Bright
○ Golden
○ Hot
○ Neon
○ Shocking
○ Sunny
○ Tropical

Signature colour

Yellow

Typical features

Hair

○ Jet black
○ Deep golden brown
○ Fiery red
○ Bright orange

Eyes

○ Deep black
○ Fiery brown
○ Bright amber
○ Turquoise
○ Sky blue
○ Emerald green

Skin

○ Porcelain
○ Off-white
○ Warm beige
○ Golden brown
○ Deep rust
○ Espresso brown

Lips

○ Cherry red
○ Beige-nude
○ Peachy pink

Some colours in the Bright Spring palette

Blues

- ○ Royal blue
- ○ Teal
- ○ Cornflour

Greens

- ○ Sea green
- ○ Grass green

Yellows

- ○ Mango
- ○ Gold

Oranges

- ○ Saffron
- ○ Apricot
- ○ Papaya

Reds

- ○ Carmine
- ○ Chestnut red
- ○ Tomato

Pinks

- ○ Neon pink
- ○ Watermelon

Purples

- ○ Dark orchid
- ○ Bright lilac
- ○ Reddish violet

True Spring

This is the warmest of the springs. They are defined by their golden glow and medium brightness and lightness.

Ranking

1. Warm
2. Medium-light
3. Medium-bright

Contrast

Medium-high

Key words

- Bright
- Coral
- Fruit
- Golden
- Honey
- Tropical
- Warm

Signature colour

Green

Typical features

Hair

- Honey brown
- Warm orange
- Golden blonde
- Honey blonde
- Strawberry blonde

Eyes

- Warm brown
- Warm amber
- Turquoise green
- Emerald green
- Sea green

Skin

- Porcelain
- Cream
- Peachy pink
- Warm beige
- Champagne
- Golden
- Honey brown
- Deep caramel

Lips

- Peach
- Peachy pink
- Rose red
- Burnt peach

Some colours in the True Spring palette

Blues

- ○ Turquoise
- ○ Sea blue

Greens

- ○ Apple green
- ○ Pale teal
- ○ Jungle green

Yellows

- ○ Vanilla
- ○ Pale banana

Oranges

- ○ Tangerine
- ○ Faded orange

Reds

- ○ Coral
- ○ Orange red
- ○ Tomato

Pinks

- ○ Watermelon
- ○ Flamingo
- ○ Salmon

Purples

- ○ Amethyst
- ○ Orchid

Light Spring

This is the lightest of the springs. They are defined by their low contrast and pastel features. They give off a warm, honey, sandy glow.

Ranking

1. Light
2. Warm
3. Soft (for a spring)

Contrast

Low

Key words

○ Floral
○ Light
○ Pastel
○ Peaches and cream
○ Warm

Signature colour

Peach

Typical features

Hair

○ Light orange
○ Strawberry blonde
○ Honey blonde
○ Yellow
○ Cream

Eyes

○ Turquoise green
○ Mint green
○ Greeny blue
○ Sky blue
○ Blue-grey

Skin

○ Porcelain
○ Off white
○ Cream
○ Vanilla

Lips

○ Peach
○ Salmon
○ Bubble gum pink
○ Peachy nude
○ Beige nude

Some colours in the Light Spring palette

Blues
○ Pale blue
○ Soft teal

Greens
○ Seafoam
○ Light apple green

Yellows
○ Light gold
○ Light saffron

Oranges
○ Soft salmon
○ Sunset orange
○ Tomato

Reds
○ Watermelon
○ Coral

Pinks
○ Light coral
○ Soft magenta
○ Warm nude

Purples
○ Lilac
○ Wisteria

Light Summer

This is the lightest of the summers. They are defined by their light, ashy features.

Ranking

1. Light
2. Cool
3. Bright (for a summer)

Contrast

Low

Key words

- Ashy
- Blossom
- Dusty
- Pastel
- Pearl
- Soft

Signature colour

Pink

Typical features

Hair

- Ice-white
- Cream
- Cool blonde
- Ashy blonde
- Dirty blonde
- Light, ashy brown

Eyes

- Turquoise
- Mint green
- Sky blue
- Icy blue
- Blue-grey
- Light grey

Skin

- Porcelain
- Off white
- Ashy
- Pinky nude

Lips

- Rose pink
- Soft peach
- Pinky nude
- Purpley nude

Some colours in the Light Summer palette

Blues

- ○ Dusty navy
- ○ Periwinkle
- ○ Cloudy blue

Greens

- ○ Light teal
- ○ Grey green

Yellows

- ○ Pale soft banana

Oranges

- ○ Light pinky peach

Reds

- ○ Soft watermelon
- ○ Light rose red

Pinks

- ○ Blush pink
- ○ Dirty pink

Purples

- ○ Soft rosy purple
- ○ Greyish purple

True Summer

True Summers are the coolest of the summers. They are defined by their gentle and mermaid-like palette.

Ranking

1. Cool
2. Medium-soft
3. Medium-light

Contrast

Medium-low

Key words

- Blush
- Cool
- Dusty
- Mermaid
- Metallic
- Soft

Signature colour

Blue

Typical features

Hair

- Ashy brown
- Mousy brown
- Mushroom brown
- Cool brown

Eyes

- Cool blue
- Blue-grey
- Mushroom grey
- Light grey
- Slate grey

Skin

- Porcelain
- Cool white
- Ashy
- Cool beige

Lips

- Rose pink
- Ballet pink
- Pinky nude
- Purpley nude
- Rose red

Some colours in the True Summer palette

Blues

○ Cornflour

○ True blue

○ Dark dusty denim

Greens

○ Soft forest green

○ Cool seafoam

○ Cool teal

Reds

○ Soft watermelon

○ Soft maroon

Pinks

○ Soft pink

○ Pale magenta

○ Dusty ballet pink

Purples

○ Lavender

○ Blueish purple

○ Icy purple

Soft Summer

Soft Summers are the softest and darkest of the summers. They are defined by their ashy features.

Ranking

1. Soft
2. Cool
3. Dark (for a summer)

Contrast

Low

Key words

- Ashy
- Dusty
- Cool
- Metallic
- Moody
- Powdery

Signature colour

Mauve

Typical features

Hair

- Dirty blonde
- Cool beige
- Mousy brown
- Cool brown
- Chocolate brown

Eyes

- Light hazel
- Olive green
- Light mushroom brown
- mushroom grey
- Light grey.
- Grey-green
- Slate grey
- Deep grey
- Blue-grey

Skin

- Off white
- Beige
- Mushroom brown

Lips

- Rose pink
- Pinky beige
- Soft red

Some colours in the Soft Summer palette

Blues

- ○ Dusty denim
- ○ Greyish teal
- ○ Lavender grey

Greens

- ○ Deep sage
- ○ Greyish khaki
- ○ Soft forest green
- ○ Faded jade

Reds

- ○ Dusky rose
- ○ Cool brownish red

Pinks

- ○ Soft raspberry
- ○ Light mauve
- ○ Oyster pink

Purples

- ○ Dusty lavender
- ○ Stormy purple

Soft Autumn

Soft Autumns are the softest and lightest of the autumns. They are defined by their honey colouring.

Ranking

1. Soft
2. Warm
3. Light (for an autumn)

Contrast

Low-medium

Key words

○ Caramel
○ Honey
○ Sandy

Signature colour

Khaki

Typical features

Hair

○ Honey blonde/brown
○ Sandy blonde
○ Dirty blonde
○ Dirty strawberry blonde

○ Reddish brown
○ Caramel blonde
○ Bronde

Eyes

○ Amber
○ Mushroom brown
○ Light hazel
○ Soft green
○ Green/blue-grey

Skin

○ Porcelain
○ Peach
○ Warm beige
○ Golden brown
○ Rich brown

Lips

○ Peach
○ Peachy pink/beige
○ Rose red
○ Muted red
○ Warm beige
○ Honey brown

Blues

○ Greyish teal

○ Soft denim

Greens

○ Soft teal

○ Camouflage green

○ Warm khaki

○ Soft yellow green

Yellows

○ Sandy yellow

○ Soft saffron

○ Light mustard

Oranges

○ Dusty salmon

○ Pale copper

Reds

○ Pale terracotta

○ Soft chestnut red

Pinks

○ Dusty peach

○ Chestnut pink

○ Champagne

Purples

○ Rose taupe

True Autumn

True Autumns are the warmest of the Autumns. They are defined by their fiery tones and medium contrast.

Ranking

1. Warm
2. Medium-soft
3. Medium-dark

Contrast

Medium-low

Key words

- Autumnal
- Coppery
- Fiery
- Pumpkin
- Rusty

Signature colour

Orange

Typical features

Hair

- Fiery red
- Deep orange
- Copper brown
- Rust red
- Bright orange
- Ginger-brown
- Rust brown
- Warm brown
- Toffee brown

Eyes

- Amber
- Caramel
- Fiery brown

Skin

- Cream
- Warm beige
- Caramel brown
- Reddish brown
- Cinnamon brown
- Coffee brown

Lips

- Peach
- Warm beige
- Burnt red
- Rose red

Some colours in the True Autumn palette

Blues

- ○ Rich teal

Greens

- ○ Olive green
- ○ Warm khaki
- ○ Yellow green

Yellows

- ○ Deep sunny yellow
- ○ Warm mustard

Oranges

- ○ Copper
- ○ Rich gold
- ○ Whisky
- ○ Brandy orange

Reds

- ○ Orange red
- ○ Deep chestnut

Pinks

- ○ Terracotta peach
- ○ Brownish pink

Purples

- ○ Soft plum
- ○ Smoky topaz
- ○ Aubergine

Dark Autumn

Dark Autumns are the deepest and brightest of the autumns. They are defined by their warm, rich tones.

Ranking

1. Dark
2. Warm
3. Bright (for an autumn)

Contrast

Medium

Key words

- Berry
- Burned
- Deep
- Fiery
- Rich

Signature colour

Red

Typical features

Hair

- Coffee brown
- Chocolate brown
- Deep espresso black
- Jet black

Eyes

- Deep amber
- Deep hazel
- Coffee brown
- Chestnut brown
- Reddish brown
- Maroon
- Deep brown

Skin

- Off white
- Cream
- Warm beige
- Toffee brown
- Warm chocolate brown

Lips

- Maroon
- Deep red
- Warm beige
- Deep peach

Some colours in the Dark Autumn palette

Blues

- Deep greyish teal

Greens

- Army green
- Forest green

Yellows

- Rich gold
- Warm mustard

Oranges

- Burnt orange
- Deep rust

Reds

- Maroon
- Wine
- Claret
- Watermelon

Pinks

- Carmine pink
- Deep rose

Purples

- Warm grape
- Deep plum

Other style systems and resources

There are dozens of what I call 'style systems': methods of defining your style based on appearance or personality categories. I can't cover all of them in one book; however, I want to share some of the key systems that have made the biggest difference to my personal style. There are many other style experts doing great things too, so feel free to do your own research, using the below resources to get started.

Belle Northrup and Harriet McJimsey

In the 1930s, the professor Belle Northrup published an article introducing the concept of yin and yang in fashion and beauty. She introduced female style archetypes based on this theory of a soft,

delicate, light (yin) vs structured, bold and strong (yang) style that is at the core of many of the following style principles. Harriet T. McJimsey in the 1960s then further developed this concept, using yin and yang to identify what are referred to as the six 'essences': dramatic, natural, classic, gamine, romantic and ingenue. The theories of these two women are the foundation of modern style systems movements.

Color Me Beautiful

Colour Me Beautiful by Carole Jackson was the one of the first published works to bring the above essences into the mainstream, in addition to popularising the notion of 'winter' 'autumn' 'spring' and 'summer' – the Colour Season categories that helps you find your best colours (page 134). Today, Colour Me Beautiful is an organisation with a directory of image consultants where you can learn how to become a stylist based on these principles.

Kibbe body types

In the 1980s David Kibbe published the book *Metamorphosis* in which he expands the essences and identifies 10–12 Image IDs (colloquially known as 'Kibbe body types'). This system took the world by storm and had a renaissance in the 2010s–2020s due to the popularity of his exclusive Facebook group. His Image IDs are based on levels of yin and yang balance. This system is what started it all for me; David Kibbe's passion for styling and his unique aesthetic elements combined with fit and flattering shapes is fascinating.

His system is delightfully complex, but I have done my best to distil the IDs/body types here.

○ **Dramatic:** This ID tends to have narrow frames, a straight figure and appear long. This type might wear tailored and straight silhouettes.

○ **Soft Dramatic:** This ID tends to be narrow, have soft figures and appear long. This type might wear lush, glamorous, large and rounded lines.

○ **Flamboyant Natural:** This ID tends to have wide shoulders, a straight figure and appear long. This type might wear deconstructed, flowing and long lines.

○ **Soft Natural:** This ID tends to have wide shoulders, a soft figure and appear slightly short. This type might wear flowing yet rounded silhouettes.

○ **Dramatic Classic:** This ID tends to appear neither particularly long nor short and have some sharpness in their frame. This type might wear moderate, even and balanced lines with just a touch of sharpness.

○ **Soft Classic:** This ID tends to appear slightly short with some soft rounded shapes to their frame. This type might wear moderate, balanced, clean lines with a soft, elegant touch.

- **Flamboyant Gamine:** This ID tends to appear petite, have contrasted shapes and have a slight sharpness to their frame. This type might wear short, straight and contrasted shapes, like pattern and high levels of detail.

- **Soft Gamine:** This ID tends to appear petite, have contrasted shapes and have a slight softness to their frame. This type might wear short, crisp, rounded silhouettes and contrasted shapes like pattern and high levels of detail.

- **Theatrical Romantic:** This ID tends to appear petite, have a narrow, column-like frame with soft, rounded shapes. This type might wear short, glamorous, sensual styles.

- **Romantic:** This ID tends to appear petite and have a notably rounded and soft frame. This type might wear soft fabrics, round shapes and fitted silhouettes.

If you would like to expand your learning and read about Kibbe body types in more depth I would recommend joining the following groups:

- Strictly Kibbe (Facebook)

- Freely Kibbe (Facebook)

- r/Kibbe (reddit)

- r/DressForYourBody (reddit)

Kitchener essences

John Kitchener's system is famous for adding the 'ethereal' category to the essence system. His system focuses strongly on facial features to help find your best lines.

- **Dramatic:** This type has structured, intense facial features that are complemented by bold, tailored styles.

- **Natural:** This type has angular, irregular and blunt facial features that are complemented by relaxed and deconstructed styles.

- **Gamine:** This type has contrasted facial features, with small yet sharp lines, that are complemented by boyish, playful styles.

Classic: This type has even, balanced and moderate facial features that are complemented by simple, clean and timeless styles.

○ **Ingenue:** This type has round, delicate and small facial features that are complemented by sweet, youthful and girlish styles.

○ **Romantic:** This type has round and lush facial features that are complemented by sensual, glamorous and womanly styles.

○ **Ethereal:** This type has long yet soft facial features that appear ageless (like the elves in *The Lord of the Rings*), which are complemented by celestial, otherworldly styles.

Color Your Style by David Zyla

In this useful book, Zyla helps you identify a few key colours by pulling directly from your features. These colours are then used to build the foundation of your wardrobe. Depending on your mood (whether romantic or tranquil, for example) Zyla will then help you find your best colour.

Your Style Key by Rita

Rita's quadrant system helps you identify the motivations behind what you buy and what makes you truly happy with your personal style. There are four types: amethyst, sapphire, ruby and moonstone, under which there are various archetypes. Once you identify your type, you'll have a better understanding of the changes you need to make in order to see getting dressed as fulfilling exercise.

Body Geometry by Merriam Style

Merriam's YouTube channel was the first to introduce me to the world of style systems. Merriam has her own version of yin and yang body types that focus on the bone structure of both body and face, as well as a four-season colour system that focuses on warm/cool and bright/soft only.

Wear It Well by Allison Bornstein

In *Wear it Well*, Borstein proposes a three-word system when it comes to personal style – this means identifying three words that will guide your style. For example, my three words are: simple, eclectic and delicate.

Put it *all*
TOGETHER

Where to begin?

Now you have an idea of your Style Roots, (page 22) your Body Matrix (page 102), and your Colour Seasons (page 141), this is the point at which it can feel a little overwhelming. Some of the things you have learned about yourself might contradict each other; perhaps you have a rounded body, but like the straight, structured styles of the Mountain Style Root (page 30).

First, it's important to remember these are all just tools – and you can choose which tool to pick up each day. Some days I desperately want to wear bright red and so I don't pick up the Colour Seasons tool that day. Whereas on public, no-makeup days, my best colours feel much more important. In the months where my weight changes, I lean on my Body Matrix a lot more so I can dress to feel my best. You get the idea.

However, some of you will want to do all of it, all the time. Although this is a lot of pressure to put on yourself, I get it. I see this as the north star to follow, especially when shopping. When you stick to your lines and your roots, you tend to buy things that last, slot nicely into your existing wardrobe and create a more unique collection of clothing. But with all these different pieces of information, where on earth do you begin?

Curating your core wardrobe

It is time to reframe how you see your wardrobe. Most of us see our closets merely as a place to store our clothing, or something to wrestle through every morning. It is much better to convert your wardrobe itself into one of the tools in your toolbox. The purpose of your wardrobe is not to just to keep your clothes in, but to make the process of getting dressed more efficient and to provide you with better outfits. Many of you may have cleared your wardrobe out in the past and found you are much better dressed during the weeks that follow (until it becomes cluttered once more!). Here, I break down some key methods for organising your wardrobe, making it a happier, healthier and more usable space.

Your key words

For each of the systems I outline in this book, I included a set of key words. Some of these will complement each other, some will contradict each other. I want you to review the keywords for your chosen Style Roots (page 22), Body Matrix lines (page 102) and Colour Seasons (page 141). Write them all down in one long list.

I now want you to highlight the words that crop up twice. This is a really easy way to distil the recommendations from each of your 'tools'.

In a different colour, work through the list and highlight the key words you really like. If you're not sure, highlight the ones you know you already like to incorporate into your outfits, or would be excited to do so.

Next, try to split all the highlighted words on the list into 'themes' (descriptive words) and 'elements' (features you could pinpoint on an item of clothing or outfit). You can now use these two lists to guide your wardrobe choices and your shopping habits.

I am narrow, short and round, a True Summer, with Flower, Mushroom and Earth Style Roots. These are some words that came up twice for me and the ones I like the most.

Key themes:

- Country
- Delicate
- Dreamy
- Eclectic
- Elegant
- Flowing
- Neutral
- Rounded
- Simple
- Soft

Key elements:

- Animal print
- Broderie anglaise
- Clean lines
- Fringe
- Midi skirt
- Pastel tones
- Polka dot pattern
- Round neckline
- Tie waist

The three-tier editing system

For lots of people, finding out your Style Roots, Body Matrix or Colour Season is a reason to buy an entirely new wardrobe, to which I say, woah slow down! You have learned and absorbed a lot of new information and it can take a while to sink in. The second reason I think you shouldn't rush to the mall is that the point of learning these systems is to help narrow down your current wardrobe and give it deeper focus – not to add more stuff to it! Eventually, you can make your way to the shops, but not until you have got to grips with your own closet.

The three-tier editing system helps you to organise your clothes into different groups or 'rings'. The basic principle is to have your core wardrobe comprised of your best pieces, and to slowly replace the imperfect pieces with those that more closely align with your style goals. As one piece comes in, an imperfect piece goes out. You don't need to throw every piece away that isn't perfect! There are lots of reasons you might want to keep items that are not technically perfect. This helps with one of my shopping rules: every piece I buy must replace one I already own, therefore *has* to be better than a piece already in my wardrobe. This rule might not be for you if you have a small wardrobe, but it's an example of how this system can be used.

Go through each piece in your wardrobe and sort it into one of the ring categories. You can do this physically, organising them into piles and reorganising your wardrobe accordingly, or you can do so digitally using a wardrobe tracking app like Whering, Indyx or Open Wardrobe.

Inner ring: Your perfect pieces

These are the pieces that are perfect. They accommodate your Body Matrix, sit within your Colour Seasons and have elements of all three of your Style Roots. There is nothing about these pieces that goes against what you have learned about yourself in this book. Sometimes these pieces aren't your most-loved, but they bring everything else together. I like to make a simple checklist to help me decide if something belongs in my inner ring. Mine looks something like this:

○ Simple
○ Waist definition
○ Touch of delicate
○ Intricate
○ Soft pink/blue/green/ off-white/grey
○ Touch of eclectic

If the item has all these elements, it probably belongs in my inner ring.

Think of the inner ring as a new and better interpretation of your 'basics'. The pieces that root the rest of your wardrobe don't have to be plain or neutral. Your perfect pieces should operate as a capsule wardrobe: they should all be in the same colour palette, have patterns that complement one another and silhouettes that melt together. (There is no reason why camel, white and black should be the better basis of a mix-and-match wardrobe than aubergine, green and tan.)

Some of my inner ring pieces include:

○ Kid's denim waistcoat

○ Blue and white striped '80s-inspired midi skirt

○ Cool-beige, suede cowboy boots

○ Cream cardigan with lace trim

○ Off-white broderie anglaise camisole

○ Flared, high-waisted jeans

○ Sheer floral shirt that contains all my best colours

○ Off-white espadrilles

○ Cool-beige trench coat

Middle ring: Almost there

These are the pieces that have an element that is perfect, but don't hit all the stops. For example, the silhouette might be perfect for your body type, but it's a colour that isn't your season. Perhaps the colour is almost the right pink but it's a bit too bright, the shape is almost right but digs in slightly at the wrong place, the style hits one of your Style Roots but not all of them. It's headed in the right direction, so it falls in your middle ring.

The idea with middle-ring items is that over time you will replace them with perfect pieces, and in the meantime, you will always aim to pair them with inner ring pieces.

Outer ring: Clothes to store

Your outer ring is for items that shouldn't be found in your day-to-day wardrobe. These are the items you should keep, but store separately.

I find that practical wear and workout gear can distort your vision for your wardrobe. Ideally, you should work towards choosing practical items that work for your Body Matrix and Colour Seasons but, even so, setting these items apart helps for clarity of day-to-day dressing.

Extremely formal wear should also be kept somewhere else. I do think you should push the boundaries on what you consider formal and try to wear these items more casually, but for the most part it helps to keep prom, bridesmaids or wedding dresses out of the mix.

Clothes that are a little too big or small go in this category. I believe giving yourself a little flexibility for weight change is important (don't throw out your whole wardrobe because you've gained/lost a little weight!) so just store these items somewhere else for now. Do note, this is different from clothes you love that have never fitted you and never will because they are built in a way that does not fit your frame.

Finally, the sentimental pieces. I am like you: I can't get rid of the graphic tee I wore every day as a teenager. It means too much to me. I am a collector of clothing because I am passionate about it, and always have been. Some of you can throw away clothes with reckless abandon – that's great. But for those of us with this irrational sentimentality, I say keep them. Just don't keep them with your regular clothes. I encourage you to put them somewhere accessible, set a date in your calendar, and visit those items once a year so you can really enjoy them. Maybe you don't even need to keep the whole item and you can cut a piece of the fabric for a scrapbook with a photo. It's okay to be sentimental. The pieces you buy should feel sentimental because they should say something about you.

Everything else ...

Any item of clothing you have that doesn't sit within these three rings probably doesn't belong in your wardrobe. If it doesn't fit and never will, doesn't work for your Body Matrix, Style Roots or Colour Season, it doesn't feel deeply sentimental and it isn't an important practical item – it should go.

This can be painful. I have bought pieces in a charity shop that I seized for their potential but never wore. Finds like this are particularly hard to part with. Over time, I've noticed that items I loved 'in the moment' often had no connection to my existing wardrobe. When shopping, these items seemed brilliant, exciting, and inspiring but, once in my wardrobe among my other clothes, my love for them faded and they were rarely worn. My mantra for shopping applies to your own wardrobe too: 'it's nice for someone, just not me'. Clothing can be appreciated without causing chaos in your wardrobe.

I also find that getting rid of an item is like admitting a failure:

I was wrong, it's not meant for my forever wardrobe, I actually hate it. There's nothing worse. But remember, growth is not failure – coming to terms with mistakes is a sign of your maturity, and it's okay to let those mistakes go (you don't need them haunting you in your closet!).

You can also take a little advice from Marie Kondo if you struggle to part with your items: hold it close, thank it for how it's served you, then let it go. If this feels a little too intense for you, just take a second to be grateful for it and let yourself move on.

Item assimilation

In theory, you should be able to pull any two or three pieces from your inner ring and create a cohesive outfit, but what about the items in your other rings? The items in your middle and outer rings are not designed to seamlessly work together as they are imperfect or sentimental.

It can be tempting to wear your imperfect pieces together and see it as an 'off' day. The result of this is an outfit that doesn't make you feel or look your best. It is likely that items in your middle and outer rings make up the bulk of your wardrobe, in which case you want to get your cost per wear of these items higher.

I like to practise item assimilation: this is where you take an item from your middle or outer rings that you want to style and pair it with your perfect pieces from your inner ring.

If the colour of the item isn't in your season, try to pair it with a tonal or opposite colour from your inner ring that *is* in your season. I love leopard print, but it often comes in warm orangey tones that don't work for my features (I need cool tones) nor the palette in my wardrobe. To solve this, I pair it with items from my inner ring that are cream, red and pink (which are complementary to my features). These colours are next to orange in the colour wheel and will make the leopard pop without contrasting my own features.

If the item is too baggy for your frame, try to balance the overall shape of the outfit using an item from your inner ring. If I wear a baggy t-shirt from my middle ring, I pair it with some slim trousers and high heels from my inner ring.

How to get rid of clothes sustainably

There is no skirting around the issue that the world is facing a serious problem with overconsumption of clothing. One of the main reasons I overthink the clothes-buying process is because it deserves that level of thought. I hope that by following this system of managing your wardrobe, you will already be doing your bit to tackle the problem.

You can also think about buying second hand, wearing more natural fibres, looking for garments made in recycled fibres and buying from companies with high principles in sustainable manufacture and distribution.

Getting rid of clothes is not easy either. There is almost no way to buy or dispose of clothing that won't have some negative impact on the planet, so it is worth considering the options.

○ One of the best methods of getting rid of clothes is to sell them or give them to friends. This gives the item new life and ensures it gets several more wears before it ends up in landfill. By having a go at selling the piece yourself on Depop, Vinted or even at a car boot sale, you are taking responsibility for the item, and it is much more likely to end up with someone who will get use out of it.

○ Another option is to pack up your clothes and send them to a clothing bank or a charity shop (or a thrift store in the US). The issue here is that charity shops are already very full, so sometimes these items go to landfill anyway.

- ○ If the item is very worn out and you would feel uncomfortable trying to sell it, it's probably not good enough for the charity shop either. If an item has stains, rips or the fabric is worn, simply turn it into rags for cleaning, or upcycle it into something else.

- ○ Similarly, you can take your clothing to specific textile recycling bins at recycling centres (they often have them outside big supermarkets too). These textiles are often shredded and used in things like insulation and padding.

- ○ The worst way to dispose of clothing is to put it in the regular bin – it will go to landfill. (I naively used to assume that whoever collected my bins sorted through my waste and disposed of it appropriately – unfortunately it is not that simple.)

My dad is the sustainable clothing king. He wears the same seven items of clothing every year, almost never washes them, wears the same jumpers he was wearing when I was born, turns everything into painting/outdoor clothes once they're tatty, then into rags once they're completely worn out. He was born in the late 1950s to a poor family, and the thriftiness of his upbringing has never left him. I don't expect you to be as committed to re-wearing your clothes as my dad, but he's a great example of why you probably don't need to buy new jeans every year. This is also a lesson in buying BETTER — if you buy high-quality clothes made with hard-wearing fabrics they will last longer, and you won't need to replace things so often.

How to organise your clothes

The order in which you place your items on your rails can make an enormous impact on your daily routine. In addition to the three-tier editing system (page 176), the following tips will help you *see* and *use* all your clothes.

1. Organise by colour

Colour is one of the first elements your eye processes, so organising clothes by colour and tone makes it much easier to locate pieces. I also find that colour makes the biggest impact when putting an outfit together, so having your wardrobe organised this way helps you to prioritise your Colour Season (page 134). Organising your clothes by colour also helps you to pinpoint pieces that stand out negatively, in other words, the items that don't meld seamlessly into the colour palette you have curated. Doing this is as simple as it sounds – just group your clothes by colour. However, do remember to think about tone, so whether an item is warm or cool. For example, a cool pink might be better placed near cool purples than reds. I like to organise my clothes like a rainbow, starting from warm yellow through orange, pink, green (and so on) to cool blue, then place my neutrals together at the end.

2. Hang rather than fold (when possible)

Almost all my clothes are now hung rather than folded. Up until recently, this wasn't possible as I had limited space, so you'll have to adapt based on how much wardrobe space you have.

The 60/30/10 rule. This is a rule often used in interior design and film theory, but it can also apply to your outfits and your wardrobe. If you are still finding none of your clothes complement each other, try to narrow down your wardrobe to three main colours. Just because your Colour Season provides you with a wealth of colours that suit you, doesn't mean you need all of them in your wardrobe. Narrow your scope and try to select the three main colours in your wardrobe (mine are off-white, pink and blue). Now choose roughly 60% of your wardrobe to be one colour, 30% to be the second colour and 10% to be the third colour. This way, your wardrobe is rooted in two main bases and one pop.

It is easy to prioritise hanging formal dresses, coats and other long clothes; however, this isn't particularly helpful on a day-to-day basis. If possible, buy a clothes rail and place it somewhere else in the room, or in a separate room (or even the garage/basement) to store the items you don't wear regularly but which need hanging. Now you can prioritise the hanging space in your main wardrobe for your inner ring (page 177), in other words, the clothes you want to wear every day. When your clothes are hung, it is easier rifle through them and locate them.

3. Buy velvet hangers

You may have heard this one before, but there is nothing more life-changing than converting all your hangers to velvet ones. One of the greatest forms of wardrobe frustration we face is having clothes slip off the edges of hangers, piling on the bottom of the wardrobe. Plastic, wooden or metal hangers often take up a lot of space, meaning you're not making full use of your wardrobe. Velvet hangers are narrow, maximising your wardrobe space, and they grab onto your clothes, meaning no slippage.

4. Separate your clothes into seasonal wardrobes

As you transition between warm and cold periods (if you live in a seasonal country), store the clothes you will wear the least outside of your wardrobe. This can be in boxes on top of your wardrobe, in vacuum-packed bags under your bed, or wherever seems most appropriate in your home. When you get your clothes out again when the weather changes, you will be surprised at how many items you had forgotten you had – it can feel like shopping but it's your own wardrobe!

5. Organise digitally

I input all my items of clothing into various wardrobe apps so that I can easily experiment with them. My favourite apps are Open Wardrobe and Whering. I also use a spreadsheet made by the creator @blondebrokeandbougie that helps you track the cost-per-wear of your items. The purpose of uploading all your clothes into these apps is so you can get a bird's eye view of your wardrobe. You can pull up items of clothing easily and quickly create an outfit around them. You can plan outfits weeks in advance, create sub-wardrobes, and track which pieces you wear the most. It can take a whole afternoon to take pictures of all your clothing and label them but, in my experience, it is so worth it.

6. Pull keystone pieces to represent your current inspiration

I often find myself lost in a storm of sudden inspiration, usually manifesting in me adding hundreds of images to my style mood boards. As much as I think mood boarding is important, at some point you have to move that inspiration into the real world. One of the best ways to do this is to select five to ten keystone pieces from your existing wardrobe – you are looking for the items that most closely match the patterns and tones you see on your mood board. For example, at the moment I have a lot of leopard print, fur and denim on my mood boards, so I've selected five to ten pieces from my wardrobe that align with this. Put these keystone pieces somewhere you can see them everyday, then build your outfits around them. See it as a challenge and let yourself be inspired. When you move into a new 'era' you can simply slot these pieces back into the wardrobe and select some new keystone items. This is essentially a reminder of the fluidity and potential of your existing wardrobe. Rather than jumping to buy something new, you should reframe how you view the clothes you already own.

7. Print your mood board and stick it inside your wardrobe door

When getting dressed, we can get so overwhelmed by the choices we have to make that we forget what we even like to wear. By placing photos of your dream outfits on the door of your wardrobe, it can help you to re-centre and plan accordingly. You could also put photos of your own outfits that you have loved in the past to remind you of what your wardrobe can achieve.

8. Control accessibility

I like to apply a method that James Clear outlines in his book *Atomic Habits.* When discussing how to stop snacking throughout the day, he suggests limiting *accessibility.* In practical terms, this means placing the things you would rather not eat in a high-up cupboard that you can't comfortably reach, and reversely placing fruit in an easily accessible place, like the kitchen table. This principle can be applied to your wardrobe. Anything that doesn't help you achieve your style goals should be placed out of reach. Things you want to wear more (because they align with your goals, have a high cost-per-wear or make you feel good) should be placed within easy reach. Often, the things we find ourselves drawn to are not the things we truly like to wear, but the things that are easy to grab in the morning. Since organising my wardrobe this way, I have found that I have gone from wearing black jogging bottoms almost everyday to one or two times in the past 365 days – it works.

How to shop

What am I missing?

Now that you have organised your wardrobe, you will be better able to pinpoint what is missing. Your wardrobe is a bit like a puzzle; you are trying to find pieces that easily slot together. In reality, your wardrobe will probably never feel complete – I know mine doesn't yet – but you can take steps to get it to a place where outfits fall out of it seamlessly.

I largely view my wardrobe in 'sets' that I am collecting. These sets are based on the core neutrals I want to see in my wardrobe:

○ Mushroom brown

○ Cool sand-beige/oatmeal

○ Off white

○ Pinky nude

○ Cool silver

○ Denim blue

An easy way to choose your neutrals is to pull colours and tones from your head hair, eyebrows or eyelashes. Refer to your Colour Season too.

For each of these colours, I would like to see one item of each of the below in my wardrobe:

○ Winter coat

○ Light jacket

○ Blazer

○ Top

○ Trousers

○ Pair of flat shoes

○ Pair of heels

○ Pair of boots

○ Handbag

○ Evening bag

This makes 54 items that seamlessly blend. My 'basics' if you will. Of course, all these items would ideally need to qualify for my inner ring, so also have elements of each of my Style Roots and accommodate my Body Matrix. I wouldn't necessarily wear each of these sets all at once (for instance, all mushroom brown items: coat, shoes, bag, trousers and top), so you don't *need* all the items for every colour set. However, it is incredibly frustrating having the perfect nude heels with no evening bag to match or complement them when you really need one. It is much easier to start with one or two neutral sets, and to collect your items one or two at a time. I spent many years building sets of basics in colours all the magazines and Pinterest boards swore to me were the classic ones: black, white and tan. However, none of these colours suits me, so I have lots of great items in colours that limit me – which is very annoying and wasteful!

Having a coat in your best colours is especially important as in winter they are, essentially, your entire outfit when you leave the house. And yet, many people choose not to invest money or time in a coat because they can be pricey, and often we simply forget about it until we really need one. Buying a coat that aligns with your Style Roots, Body Matrix and Colour Season is one of the most low-lift ways to improve your winter style.

Gaps in your wardrobe

Gaps in your wardrobe

You should now understand the concept of having 'gaps' in your wardrobe: the things you need in order to dress your best. There are a few types of gap:

○ **Any missing pieces in your 'sets' of basics** (page 190) – especially bags and shoes.

○ **Items you need to bring everything else together.** I recently realised that an animal print bag would be an easy way to add my Earth Style Root (page 42) to any plain outfit. This type of gap can also manifest as a certain type of fabric or a summer version of a winter piece you love. Colour can also be a factor here – not because it belongs to one of your sets, but because you want to add a pop of something brighter from your Colour Season.

○ **Something you have wanted for a very long time** that you are desperate to seek out.

○ **Middle ring items** (page 178). These are the items found in your wardrobe that *almost* align perfectly with your Style Roots, Body Matrix and/or Colour Season. You can slowly replace these items with others that are perfect.

○ **Perfect items that no longer fit or are worn out.** If something isn't likely to fit any time soon or it has reached the end of its life, that gap needs filling. In the same vein, you might own items that are perfect on paper, but are bad quality, uncomfortable or itchy – these will likely need replacing with a better alternative.

> Be wary of the false wardrobe gap! This is when you buy a new item that doesn't slot in seamlessly with the rest of your wardrobe. If you have to create a new 'mini wardrobe' around that one item, then it probably wasn't a good purchase.

The ultimate shopping list

Based on the gaps you've pinpointed, review your wardrobe and note down a list of the items you need to make the pieces you already own work together.

Mine looks something like this:

- My tan summer shoes but in sand
- Off-white knee-high boots
- Oatmeal tie-waist coat
- Cool-tone leopard print ankle boots
- Nude blazer
- Linen blazer
- Powdery blue winter coat
- Nude cardigan
- Nude sailor pants
- Silver leather skirt
- Off-white sunglasses
- Silver hoop earrings
- Off-white handbag
- Silver evening bag
- Knit dress like the one from the film *No Time to Die*

The reason I keep an ultimate shopping list like this is that it keeps me focused when shopping. Rather than buying something I see on a whim, or being unknowingly suckered in by a trend, I put the item on the list and it waits its turn. This gives me time to review and decide if it would be a good purchase – I only want to buy things that I am going to love and wear for years. The list is perpetual. It forces me to think about the bigger goal of creating a wardrobe that serves me, rather than rushing to find something for a party next week. The idea is not to buy everything on your list at once, but to cultivate a slower attitude to curating your wardrobe.

Hyper-practical items

One of my greatest passions is encouraging women to invest time and money into their hyper-practical wardrobes. These include some of the following items:

o Walking coat

o Raincoat

o Leggings

o Jogging bottoms

o Shorts

o Hoodies

o Vests

o Sports bra

o Hiking boots

o Wellington boots

o Running trainers

o Sandals

o Socks

o Sunhat

o Umbrella

Essentially, they are the items you have specifically to combat weather or exercise. They can also be pieces for lazing about in (your 'loungewear'). But whoever said comfy and practical pieces have to look bad? These pieces hold power because you likely wear them almost every day. If you live in the UK, like me, you probably wear your wellies and your walking coat at least twice a week in the autumn and winter. If you live somewhere really warm you will likely wear sandals, shorts and a hat most days to manage the hot weather.

Because these items have a practical purpose, many of us dismiss them out of habit. 'That's just my dog-walking coat' – wrong. That coat finds itself on your body every morning, so it *matters*. These are, in fact, the high-leverage items in your wardrobe. Not only are they

your most worn pieces, but looking good in them also says a lot about you. Because most people dismiss these items, putting some love into them says a lot about your attention to detail.

If nothing else, I would consider getting hyper-practical items in your Colour Season so they light up your face. This way you can look effortlessly stunning even in your most practical gear. Alternatively, think about aligning these pieces with your Style Roots so that they bring you joy every time you wear them.

Looking at your hyper-practical items in this new way is an easy pick-me-up. If you're wearing items that you know make you look good, even when you're just exercising or running errands, you'll *feel* good too!

The importance of saying no

Saying 'no' can be an act of self-love in the same way that saying 'yes' is. We are usually living with two sets of desires running parallel: the version of you that wants a packet of crisps and the version of you who has sworn not to snack on ultra-processed food; the version of you that wants to watch the TV and the version of you that needs to do 20 minutes of yoga so that she can actually enjoy her day. Generally, we understand that it's better to listen to the latter self, but not when it comes to fashion. With fashion, people often kid themselves that if they want it in the moment, it must be good for their style. This is not always true.

The only way to create a seamless wardrobe with clothes that help you feel your best every day is to say 'no' very regularly. Your no defines your style as much as your yes; the things you leave behind say something about your taste, your eye and your discernment.

If I didn't say no, I would have a wardrobe full of clothes that only felt 'half-right' and I would be buying twice as many items. In short, it's a waste of money and it's not kind to the planet.

I have a rule that if it's not perfect, it's not coming home with me. I think most of the time the problem stems from the lies you tell yourself because you want an item. I had this experience just the other day; I found a beautiful faux fur coat at an incredible discount. I adore fur styles for winter, it was the perfect shade of grey to light up my face and it was so cosy. I was convincing myself to buy it, but in the back of my mind there was a twinge of discomfort. I was ignoring it because I wanted the coat; if I bought the coat I would feel amazing as I left the store, and it was so almost perfect that I could wear it for a while and enjoy it. But that itch in the back of my brain could see it: the collar was too wide, and the coat was overwhelming my frame – it didn't suit my Body Matrix. It's hard to listen to the voice of reason when you find something you love because it's gutting leaving that item on the rail and walking away. However, it's even more gutting when you get an item home only to admit to yourself that you've spent £100 on something that simply doesn't look right.

The path of saying no is a patient one. Sometimes it can mean not bringing anything new into your wardrobe for weeks or even months. It means saying goodbye to items that you were excited about, that made your heart skip. Here, I come back to my mantra: 'it's nice for someone, but it's not for me'. When shopping, sometimes I will feel myself jumping for an item; because of my job, I have appreciation for clothes from various Style Roots, but that doesn't mean they belong in my wardrobe. I simply take a moment

to appreciate the item (sometimes I even whisper 'wow'), then move on. It can help to think of someone who the item would work for instead. For example, I might say 'my mum would love that bag' or 'Carys (my best friend) would look incredible in that'. Perhaps you even go ahead and buy the item for them as a gift to get you through the need to buy it.

The Yes-No Test

Ask yourself these questions when you are thinking of buying an item. If you answer YES to the first set of questions and NO to the second set of questions, then you are allowed to buy the item. Be strict with yourself and ensure you answer all the questions truthfully!

You must answer YES to ...

- Does this work for my body type?

- Does it accommodate my dominant features?

- Is this one of my best colours (or combination of best colours)?

- Does this serve a different purpose to anything I already own?

- Is this something I have been wanting recently?

- Could I wear it with five to ten other pieces in my wardrobe?

- Do I own a pair of shoes that will go with this item?

- Does it work for my Style Roots? Or does it work with two of my Style Roots and be combined with other items in my wardrobe to satisfy the third Style Root?

- Does it actually fit?

- Could I wear this item in multiple settings (you should be able to wear it in three to five of the below situations):

  - Lounging in front of the tv

  - Working at home

  - Going for a coffee/ shopping/brunch

  - Going to the pub

  - Family party

  - Going clubbing

  - Going for dinner at a local restaurant

  - Going for a dinner at a five-star restaurant/hotel

  - Going to the theatre/ opera/ballet

  - Going to a bar

You must answer NO to ...

○ Am I lying to myself, and the colour is actually almost perfect but not quite right?

○ Do I have lots of items in my wardrobe in this colour?

○ Is there something I own that does the same thing or achieves the same effect?

○ Is this something I actually want, or is it just similar (but not quite the same) to something on my ultimate shopping list (page 193) that it makes me want to give in?

○ Is there something about this piece that is obviously outside of the realm of my Style Roots/ Body Matrix/Colour Season that would throw off the rest of my wardrobe? (perhaps it is almost perfect but it has studs on the neckline that work for none of my Style Roots.)

○ Is there something jarring about the item? (Perhaps a missing button/dodgy zip/a cuff that is irritating me/an itchy fabric.)

○ Is there something negative about the item that I am deliberately ignoring?

This list of questions should help you go back and forth on whether an item is worth buying or not. Unless the piece passes all the questions above, you shouldn't bring it into your wardrobe.

What about buying second hand? Surely it's okay for an item to be slightly imperfect when it's second hand because you're saving it from landfill? It's true that there is no shortage of clothing in the world, so you have to make the choice you are most comfortable with. Personally, my wardrobe is overrun with clothing, so I only want to bring clothes into it that I am going to love wholeheartedly. If the second-hand item passes the YES-NO test then I would buy it, but if it isn't the right colour for me or it doesn't match my Style Roots it will be better loved by someone else.

The hunt

The question I struggle most with, is 'which stores work best for my Body Matrix/Style Roots/Colour Season? Unfortunately, most shops are not set up with these things in mind, so there is no one-stop shop to buy everything you need that's perfect for you. Shopping must be a process and a habit that you cultivate.

Everyone likes to shop in different ways and finds that different methods work for them, so feel free to carry on shopping in the way you enjoy, if you already enjoy it. The problem is that for many of you, shopping for clothes feels like a nasty chore and you don't trust yourself to make the right decisions. If you are this far into the book, you now have the tools to make shopping a better experience because you know what you are looking for. You can trust yourself and your ultimate shopping list (page 193). Now you can adapt your shopping mindset and think of ticking things off your list as a game or treasure hunt. This makes you shop more effectively and makes it fun!

The biggest piece of advice I can give you is to find 'the jumble'. Most people are intimidated by the jumble, but I encourage you to embrace it. The jumble is where you find treasure and where you learn to follow your instincts. My favourite sources of jumble are TK Maxx and second-hand shops, including thrift stores and charity shops. When I lived in Montreal, I was blown away by the concept of the thrift store: massive rooms – almost warehouses – full of vintage clothes. It's a concept that does not translate to the compactness of the UK, and one that I miss. Strangely, I find the jumble less intimidating than perfectly curated shops with clothes neatly lined on the shelves and rails. High street stores are also largely unhelpful because they are designed, just like supermarkets, to draw you in with goodies. The placement of the sale rails, the basics, the trend-led items and the sparkly bits are there to trip you up, just like chocolate by the counter. The jumble is designed as a jumble, and so you can follow your gut with greater ease. That's not to say I've never made a mistake in the jumble – the draw of the jumble is, of course, the bargain, so try not to get side-tracked by that. Only let the lower price tag sway you if the item is something on your ultimate shopping list and aligns with your style goals.

Note: *It's also worth confirming to yourself that it's a price you would be willing to pay for an item if it wasn't on sale.*

Similarly, avoid shopping online where possible. I despise shopping online; the item almost never fits right or looks the same as the photo, and often you can't be bothered to send it back because it's *almost* right, so it becomes a nuisance in your wardrobe. When you shop in person, you have much more control; you can feel the quality of the item, you can try it on, you can see where it snags, you can see its real colour. It's less of a gamble. Online shopping has taken over in-person shopping for a reason; it's easier. But that doesn't mean it's better.

When you shop in person, you give the high street a reason to continue, you discover independent shops, plus you can make a day of it and what you might have spent on shipping charges you can use to buy lunch. If you are going to shop online, apply the principle of the jumble and shop using second hand apps like Vinted, Depop or Vestiaire Collective.

How to buy trends

You may have guessed that I am not the biggest fan of trend-focused shopping. The tricky nature of trends is that they cleverly mask themselves behind other words like 'cool', 'modern', 'up to date'. I personally think you should aim for higher style heights than simply feeling 'current'. The other problem with trends is that they are not always obviously a trend, and it's not often easy to decide if you only like something *because* it is a trend. There are so many items that have appeared on my social media feed that I have ogled at because trends are designed to be beautiful, exciting, or unique, they *want* to grab your attention.

I don't believe that anything that's a trend is inherently bad, just as I don't believe that any item of clothing that is 'out of style' is inherently bad. However, I know in my experience that it's the trends I have jumped for that I have ended up hating again the quickest. Trends can get this shiny veil over them: the first time you see it, you think 'ugh what is that', but by the twentieth time it feels quite normal and by the thirtieth time you find that you actually kind of like it. Once you've bought it, you wear it, and you find that it quickly bores you, even repulses you, and it has to go.

The patchwork test

A trend should only find its way into your wardrobe if it aligns with your Style Roots, and this is a key way to test that. I named this test after a particular pair of jeans that became trendy during the Covid-19 pandemic. This was a period of rapid 'micro-trends' as people relied on dopamine dressing for quick rushes of pleasure. This pair of jeans in question was a patchwork of brown-burgundy and off-white denim squares, with frayed hems. For a brief moment of time, they were *everywhere*. I've used these jeans as an example below:

Pick the item apart into its defining features:

- ○ Patchwork
- ○ Frayed edges
- ○ Denim
- ○ Burgundy
- ○ Geometric pattern

Take the most dominant of these elements (patchwork in this case) and search for it on a second-hand clothing app (such as Depop or Vinted).

If you like the majority of what you see, it's a good sign that you are actually interested in this item. If you can't bear the thought of buying anything else but this one item, then it's likely this trend doesn't actually align with your style goals. If you do like the majority of what you see, consider buying one of the alternate items from Depop instead, or feel free to buy the original item.

Don't worry too much if an item you already own or find second-hand is recognisably a micro-trend — if it aligns with your Style Roots, Body Matrix, or Colour Seasons then it probably belongs in your wardrobe.

On the whole, I believe that avoiding trends allows you to achieve a unique personal style. However, once you feel a little more in control of your buying habits and know you can trust yourself to buy within your style goals, it can help to keep on top of current fashion trends.

The relationship with trends I suggest you foster is one of watchfulness. Once you have your ultimate shopping list (page 193), and an idea of your Style Roots, Body Matrix and Colour Season, you can simply watch and wait. The periwinkle purple colour that was popular one year was the perfect time for Light Springs (page 152) to fill their wardrobes with pieces that happily carried them through the trend and beyond.

The rules for when not to buy a trend

You can't wear the item with five to ten things you already own.
If you have to buy extra things in order to make this item work in your wardrobe, it's a sign that it doesn't belong there.

It doesn't match your features.
This should be obvious by now: if it doesn't work with your Colour Season or Body Matrix, it gets left behind.

It doesn't align with your current style goals. This can mean aligning with your Style Roots, or other style systems you are prioritising, but it can mean whatever feels personal to you. This also doesn't have to mean your long-term goals (for example, one of my current short-term goals is to add more Kate Moss-inspired pieces to my wardrobe).

You saw it on somebody else (real or online) and liked it. This isn't inherently a bad sign, but in isolation this isn't enough to warrant buying an item. The fact that an item looks good on an influencer or a friend doesn't mean it belongs in your wardrobe.

You disliked it a month ago. If you disliked the trend a very short period of time ago, this suggests that you have simply acclimatised to it, and you will probably revert to disliking it in the future.

You can find more than one of the same item on a second-hand app (such as Depop or Vinted) with one quick search. This one is particularly important; if people are already selling it, it's a sign that the item doesn't wear well or that it's a micro trend.

How to buy unique pieces

There is a time and a place for looking classic, elegant or expensive, but I don't believe these are the only, or most important, markers of good personal style. True timeless style is not about adopting a certain 'Parisian' aesthetic, but shopping beyond trends and cohesively expressing your personality. It is the unique items that transcend time and find their forever place in your wardrobe.

There are certain items in my wardrobe that I know will stay there for years to come, and it's not because they're my basics, it's because they mean something to me. You may have noticed through reading this book that I'm incredibly sentimental, and clothing is often at the centre of that sentimentality. I will always regret giving away my green Topshop tea-dress that I wore on my first date with my boyfriend just because I gained a bit of weight. Unlike what lots of people on social media might lead you to believe, it's the pieces that have remained in my wardrobe for more than ten years that are unique, *not* the neutral, simple pieces. These include:

○ An electric blue fur jacket that belonged to my nanny

○ A leopard print crop top

○ A plaid miniskirt

○ A fitted faux-tweed jacket

○ My mum's blue, suede military jacket from the noughties

How do you go about finding special, personality-filled pieces that you love, rather than opting for dopamine-dressing statement pieces that you will get bored of in a year?

The best route is to look at your background – draw inspiration from your own life and the things you love and are excited by. Try noting down what you love or what excites you about the different prompts below:

Pull from where you are from: Your hometown, your country, the place you grew up and the people you grew up around. Jeanne Damas, the founder of beauty and clothing brand Rouge, created her line of clothing with this in mind: she pulled from the women of France that she was inspired by growing up, and in doing so created a brand that represents the iconic, modern and timeless French woman. For me, the British countryside often finds its way into my style through tweed jackets and wellington boots.

Pull from your childhood: The toys you played with, your school uniform, your favourite colours, outfits you love looking back on. Everyone has strong feelings about their childhood, whether happy or sad, and channelling this into your style can create exciting effects.

Pull from your family: Your heritage can be an excellent place to start. Look at outfits your mum and dad wore when they were your age. Were you ever inspired by your siblings? Whether pieces are handed down to you or you buy things inspired by your family tree, they will always feel special to you.

Pull from places you have travelled to: If you are lucky enough to have travelled, colours, textures, patterns, prints, fabrics, and jewellery from other countries that have struck a chord with you can be a way of incorporating memories into your personal style.

Pull from celebrities you used to be obsessed with: Rather than focusing on the current 'it-person', look back across your lifetime and consider the celebrities, artists or models who have piqued your interest. Is there something about their style you can bring into your wardrobe?

Pull from your friends: You are the people you surround yourself with and, assuming you like your friends, it is okay to take inspiration from them sometimes. It's unlikely your friends are going to want to be copied exactly, but it is okay to buy a piece inspired by something they were wearing.

Pull from your teenage angst: So many people had an angry emo, goth or edgy phase as a teenager. There is something so appealing about expressing your depth of emotion at this age. That version of you is still in there somewhere – let her out sometimes.

Pull from music you love: This can be as abstract as you want it to be. The simplest form is: I love country music so I am going to incorporate some Western aesthetics into my style.

Pull from movies/TV shows you love: Some of my favourite TV shows and movies, like *Pretty Woman*, *Gilmore Girls* and even *Doctor Who* have had an enormous impact on my style. Think about the TV shows that have inspired you over the years and pull some nods into your wardrobe (even as a cosplay that only you would recognise).

Pull from interior design: Your home is as good a representation of your personal style as your clothing. We don't tend to overthink the things we buy for our home in the same way we do for clothes, so often our home is a useful way to look objectively at the styles and colours we are naturally drawn to.

Essentially, it's important to have your eyes and ears open to inspiration beyond what brands, social media and magazines feed you. There is so much depth to your history and personality – let your style tell that story.

Putting an outfit together

Ok, you've done all the prep. But what happens at 7.30am when you're standing in front of your wardrobe? Don't panic – putting clothes on your body is what we have been working towards.

The outfits you choose are important, as these are what tell your story. When you go to a meeting with pinky nude shoes rather than black ones, it can say something subtle about your sweet and gentle nature. When you wear the wrong colour on a first date, your brightness can be diminished. Many of us are saying things with our outfits that we don't even mean to as we are unfamiliar with the language of personal style.

It is important to note that putting an outfit on in the morning is, of course, about more than how other people see you. The purpose of putting clothes together seamlessly is to find an outfit that can support you for the day ahead. Your clothes should make you feel confident, comfortable and satisfy a creative need. You should include a healthy mix of formulaic and intuitive dressing when getting dressed – in other words, consider the tools you've learned in this book *and* the way you feel on any given day.

Something that helps me is remembering that not every outfit needs to include every aspect of my style. Perhaps one day not all your Style Roots feature in your outfit – that's fine. Your personal style is an amalgamation of all the outfits you wear, not a single outfit on a single day.

How to use your style toolbox

Once you have a wardrobe that is streamlined and curated, putting an outfit together becomes less of a challenge. A smaller number of colours, styles, silhouettes, and shapes will create stronger cohesion, which makes creating an outfit from any two pieces in your wardrobe much easier. However, there are still challenges with fusing your Style Roots, Body Matrix and Colour Season. Do you prioritise your high contrast body or your low contrast season? Your need for waist definition or flowing fabrics? Especially for those of us with contrasting features, putting an outfit together can still feel like an intimidating prospect.

Details, silhouettes and colours

A simple rule I use for combining Body Matrix, Style Roots and your Colour Season within an item or outfit goes as follows:

○ Your **Body Matrix** and lines should influence the **silhouette** of the item or outfit.

○ Your **Style Roots** should be apparent in the **details** of the item or outfit.

○ Your **Colour Season** should be represented in the **colour(s)** of the item or outfit.

Silhouette: The shape of your outfit. This includes elements like sleeve shape, neckline, where the waist falls, the shape of the trousers, the skirt length, the shoe shape.

Details: The design elements of the outfit. This includes things like patterns, adornments (bows, zips, buttons, anything 3D) and fabrics.

Colours: The colours in your outfit. Although Style Roots have a colour element, using your Colour Season as the basis for your outfits helps to streamline things.

Refine / Focus / Follow

This is a method I use to combine two different tools together. It shows how you can reframe the conflict between two tools as a relationship.

Let's say you are struggling to fuse your Body Matrix with your Style Roots. Someone who was wide, short and round might struggle with the Mountain Style Root, which encompasses items like blazers and suit trousers, items that are often better suited to straight, narrow and long frames. Let's use the example of the pointed high heel, which adds a formal, powerful feel to any outfit.

Refine: *Refine or adjust each detail so that it fits your recommendations.* For example, the shoe would become a round toed shoe with a chunky heel.

Focus: *Focus on the individual lines.* Rather than trying to force a stiletto, take the clean, patent leather element of the stiletto shoe and apply it to a shoe that better fits the wide, short and round type, like a patent chunky loafer.

Follow: *Follow your recommendations.* Rather than trying to force the stiletto into the outfit, add a Mountain feel somewhere else in the look, for example a cropped, high-waisted suit-inspired trouser with a flare leg.

Creating an effect — when to break the rules

Rather than viewing your outfits as 'good' or 'bad', 'flattering' or 'unflattering', it can help to expand your vocabulary. When you add or take elements away from an outfit, it can change the entire feel.

It probably isn't as simple as 'this outfit is bad': is it too relaxed? Does it look quirkier than you intended? Does it feel too girly? Does it feel too youthful? Do you feel more mature than you wanted? There are many assumptions out there about what someone might be trying to achieve with their outfit.

However, not everyone is trying to look traditionally beautiful, feminine or timeless. An outfit has only truly failed if it has not achieved what you wanted it to.

Dressing in harmony with your body will create a timeless, striking, beautiful look. When you dress in line with your Body Matrix, Style Roots and Colour Season you shine the most. You would probably want to dress with all three tools in mind for a job interview, a first date or when doing public speaking.

However, on certain body types, looks that are constantly preached as 'timeless' or 'classic' can appear frumpy and grandmotherly. Similarly, on certain body types, 'fun', 'playful' or 'quirky' styles might appear timeless or even bland. If your goals are to look quirky, rebellious, unusual and shocking, dressing in perfect harmony with your Body Matrix lines might not be the way to do that. If you wanted to dress more in the Moon Style Root (page 61), wearing a couple of items that are heavier, sharper or darker than your recommendations would be an effective way to create this impression. However, there is a difficult balance when you start to break the rules, as too many broken rules can make an outfit feel messy and unintentional rather than exciting. If you are a Light Summer (page 154), but want to embrace your darker side, instead of reaching straight for the colour black, move only slightly outside your season and try wearing a cool, deep purple. It will create an edginess without the harshness.

Style Roots are a good tool to help define your intentions when playing with fashion. Changing up or adding one or two subtle details from another Style Root will be enough to convey a change or shift in your outfit. You don't need to adopt every recommendation of that Style Root to achieve a certain aesthetic. For example, someone who is long, straight and narrow who wants to dip their toes into the Flower Style Root (page 49) would be able to use a simple floral print in their outfit to convey this. They wouldn't need to also wear puff sleeves, frilly ankle socks, ballet shoes and a mini bag – all of which contradicts their lines.

What makes a good outfit?

The 18 components of style

People who are style icons almost always incorporate these 18 elements into their personal style. In order to create this list, in addition to my own ideas, I asked my social media followers and clients what they think is most important when creating any stylish outfit.

Fit of clothes: Wearing clothes that aren't baggy or too tight in certain places is such a simple way to elevate your personal style.

Matching your features to your outfit: Namely dressing for your Body Matrix and Colour Season – let yourself light up!

Authenticity/matching your personality: Style Roots is a great tool to ensure your style aligns with your personality.

Uniqueness: Having an element about your style that is hard to replicate or doesn't just follow trends (this makes you someone to watch!).

Timelessness: Being trendless and wearing an outfit that could be from any era shows your style is more than just fashionable.

Balance/proportions: It doesn't matter how expensive or nice your items are, if they are placed together in a way which makes no sense, you won't appear stylish.

Courage/confidence: This can be a hard one to see at first glance, but wearing your clothes with pride, and even wearing something different from the people around you, can suggest you are comfortable in yourself and your decisions.

Cohesion: When all the elements of your outfit tell a story by having a connection.

Consistency: Stylish people have a recognisable stamp that they come back to, day after day. It might be a colour palette, silhouette, detail or even certain jewellery. This shows you know who you are and you know what you like – you're not guessing. This doesn't mean you can't experiment though!

Making a statement: This can mean wearing something bold and bright, or it can simply mean being you even when under pressure to dress a different way.

Colour: You don't have to dress in lots of bright pops of colour in order to be stylish, but being aware of your Colour Season and using that information mindfully will make your outfit more interesting.

Strong foundation: Having unique and quality basics will lift your entire wardrobe. If you have a set of items you can rely on, you will almost always walk out of the house looking stylish.

Inspiring/creativity/newness: When people see something they have never seen before, they take a moment to look

Wardrobe organisation: Having an efficient wardrobe means the style choices you make will be better every day.

Selectiveness: Say no! Being picky and selective is a clear sign of someone who has taste (page 196).

Simplicity: An outfit that can be summed up in a few words is usually a winner. This doesn't have to mean minimal or neutral. An outfit that sends a clear message and has focus is a stylish one.

Quality: This doesn't have to mean expensive! Of course, a little money helps, but remember designer clothing does not always equal quality, and nor does high street clothing equal rubbish. Well-made products with natural fabrics will elevate your wardrobe.

I really recommend Andrea Cheong's videos on TikTok for learning about where to buy your clothing.

Practicality: When you buy a summer cardigan with fur on it, you will look out of place. Similarly, wearing a ball gown to the pub feels like you are trying too hard, and wearing jeans to the opera says, 'I don't know what I am doing'. An alternate spin on this one: focus on your practical items and don't dismiss them!

Outfit templates

One of my personal style icons is Katherine, Princess of Wales (Kate Middleton). Something I realised one day while obsessing over her photos is that she wears almost the same six outfits again and again:

○ Knee-length coat dress + heels + hat/fascinator

○ Smart trousers + blazer + smart shoe

○ Jeans + blazer + flat or chunky shoe

○ Statement top + culottes + day shoe

○ Tea dress + heels

○ Flared leg trouser + heels + long coat

The way Kate dresses as the Duchess of Cambridge or the Princess of Wales is such an important part of her role. It makes sense that she would employ the 80/20 principle in her style. The 80/20 rule, or the Pareto Principle, essentially states that 80% of the success comes from 20% of the output – you can use it to find where you should double down. I would assume that these outfits are the 20% that got the most positive feedback either in the press or from witnesses, and so they come back in new iterations.

You can apply the same principle to your outfits; when you find an outfit you love, try to replicate it with other pieces in your closet. Here's how:

1. Take a picture: Record the outfit in a way that is easy to return to.

Note: *Taking pictures of your outfits is a good habit to get into! This can help you collect a record of your style; see how you are improving and get objective about your wardrobe choices.*

2. Break the outfit into its elements: What kinds of shape are you wearing? Are the trousers flared or cinched? Where does your blazer hit? How heavy are your shoes? What jewellery are you wearing?

3. Write the elements in a list:
Then see if you can recreate the same shapes with other items in your wardrobe.

4. Try to reimagine the outfit in the context of a different season:
Wedged sandals aren't going to work in the winter, but could you replace them with a wedged boot?

5. Reimagine the outfit in the context of a different formality:
What would you need to change for it to become appropriate in a different situation?

6. Think of a list of things you do regularly that you need outfits for:
For example, Kate's might include:

- ○ Going to a daytime work event like visiting a school or hospital
- ○ Attending a royal wedding
- ○ Going for a hike
- ○ Going for an important meeting

Mine include:

- ○ Working from home
- ○ Going to the pub
- ○ Going out for dinner
- ○ Walk at the beach
- ○ Going dancing

For each event, try to create your ideal outfit using clothes from your wardrobe. This can serve as the basis of your outfit templates.

Try to find between three and ten templates you can return to in order to create consistency and cohesion in your style.

Becoming confident with your style

When I was thirteen, I had a very playful attitude to fashion. I had a book where I created fashion collages, I obsessed over the outfits in my favourite movies like *Mean Girls* and *The Devil Wears Prada* and I bought cheap, colourful makeup. Of course, not everyone was as lucky as I was to have the freedom to play with clothes however I liked, but I think we should all have more of the thirteen-year-old spirit: doing what we can within our budget, reimagining the clothes we have and being curious about our own personal style.

It was around this age that I was bullied. No one flushed my head in a toilet like I saw in American movies, but almost everyone in the school was saying nasty things about me – I was the hot topic of the day. What did I do to deserve such treatment? I dared to stand out. I came to school with clip-in purple highlights, a collection of badges on my tie, weird makeup, ripped tights and I dared to make YouTube videos about it. I tried hard in my classes, I did all the school concerts, I was the loudest singer in rehearsals even if I wasn't the best. In short, I was a naturally confident teenager and so I know first-hand how difficult and scary it can be to 'put yourself out there'. That young girl would be so excited to think that future-her is publishing a book about fashion.

One of my mantras is 'do embarrassing things'. Obviously, I still stress about 'cringe' and I get embarrassed. Being true to yourself, playing with your style and going out of your comfort zone can be really scary. It can feel vulnerable to have the real you on show. But the rewards are so worth it – and keeping this mantra in mind has brought me so much happiness. I dare you to wear what you'd consider to be an 'embarrassing' outfit – what truly is the worst that can happen?

At university, I went to a ball on a boat and my friends and I took this very literally and turned up in what were essentially prom dresses. When we arrived, almost everyone else on the boat was wearing normal clubbing dresses. My friend instantly started panicking but I said to her: 'they wish they were dressed like you'. She revealed to me months later that this had a huge impact on her and she uses the phrase frequently.

The truth is that everyone is more worried about what they look like than what you look like and deep down everyone wishes they had the confidence to dress more loudly. I know I had more fun in my slinky blue gown than I would have in any old, short clubbing dress – I probably wouldn't even remember the night otherwise.

This book requires you to absorb a lot of information, but if you take just one thing away from these pages, I hope it's the knowledge that style is a tool to show the world all the amazing things about yourself.

Dress right and show the world your best self!

Style glossary

I've included only those aesthetics and styling terms that I have mentioned in this book. There are, of course, many more – if you're interested to learn more about them I encourage you to do further research online.

Styling terms

Body Lines: Your Body Lines can refer to the shapes of your body and the clothes that mirror your best silhouettes. Your best lines are the shapes that work best on your frame.

Classic: The classic style type is simple, balanced and moderate. A classic influence usually means incorporating minimal styles, simple patterns and moderate lengths.

Details: Your outfit details are the elements that don't include the silhouette, they are the 'cherry-on-top' such as pattern, print, adornments or any 3D elements.

Dramatic: The dramatic style type is intimidating, sharp, structured. A dramatic influence usually means incorporating straight, narrow and long shapes.

Ethereal: The ethereal style type is celestial, otherworldly and angelic. An ethereal influence frequently means incorporating long yet soft shapes, and styles inspired by angels.

Gamine: The gamine style type is playful, cheeky and youthful. A gamine influence usually means incorporating unusual silhouettes, contrasted shapes and bold patterns.

Ingenue: The ingenue style type is light, airy and girlish. An ingenue influence usually means incorporating cute, rounded and small silhouettes.

Natural: The natural style type is relaxed, down-to-earth and athletic. A natural influence usually means incorporating draped, wide, slouched shapes and natural textures.

Motif: A motif is a recurring, often thematic, pattern or idea.

Romantic: The romantic style type is soft, lush and glamorous. A romantic influence usually means incorporating fitted silhouettes, large, round patterns and soft fabrics.

Yin/Yang: the scale of yin to yang is at the root of many style systems. Yin, in this context, refers to shapes whthatich are small, delicate, light, round and soft. Yang refers to shapes that are large, long, heavy, straight and sharp.

Aesthetics

Aesthetic: Style aesthetics refer to a niche, specific kind of outfit style or capsule wardrobe that has a thematic element and might connect to a visual mood board of imagery. Often these aesthetics originate from, or are popularised on, social media such as TikTok or Pinterest. Often, style aesthetics popularise an existing or nostalgic way of dressing, rebranding it from the perspective of the mainstream.

'70s boho: The 1970s provided the foundation of bohemian clothing as we know it today, incorporating tribal patterns, earthy tones, flowing fabrics and natural fibres.

Athleisure: A practical way of dressing that combines athletic wear such as leggings and hoodies with everyday clothing.

Ballet-core: Outfits inspired by the practical wear of ballerinas and ballet classes, such as leg warmers, wrap cardigans and white tights.

Beach chic: A bohemian yet expensive beach-inspired look.

Bohemian: Bohemian style can mean many things, but the style originates from a group of French artists in the 19th century, and often pulls inspiration from traditional Romanian traveller clothing.

Coastal cowgirl: A take on the coastal grandmother aesthetic (see below) that incorporates cowgirl themes such as cowboy boots, suede waistcoats and stetsons.

Coastal grandmother: This aesthetic is inspired largely by the Nancy Meyers film *Something's Gotta Give* where the seemingly wealthy, older, female main character's story plays out by the beach. The styles are neutral, minimal and effortless.

Coquette: A combination of sweet and sexy styles, the name having connotations of young, flirty women. This aesthetic is also sometimes known as 'Lolita', referencing the novel by Vladimir Nabokov.

Cottage-core: Cottage-core draws on traditional feminine, rural silhouettes and imagery, such as wicker baskets, picking flowers in a country cottage garden, linen dresses and lace up leather boots.

Dark academia: A gothic spin on traditional academic, British, Oxford/Cambridge inspired outfits and imagery. For example: tweed jackets, plaid skirts, sweater vests, pocket watches and knee-high socks.

E-girl: This aesthetic is a more colourful, somewhat feminine take on grunge styles of the 1990s and 2010s.

Emo: Short for 'emotional', emo styles pull from '90s grunge styles, including dark colours, ripped jeans and plaid skirts, but rose to popularity in the late '00s and 2010s.

French girl: Inspired by the women of Paris, often combining minimal, effortless styles with feminine, intricate details such as lace camisoles, Breton tops, ballet flats and blue denim jeans.

Gothic: Gothic pulls from styles inspired by gothic novels and architecture. This aesthetic often appears vampiric, including dark colours, intricate details and historical silhouettes.

Grunge: A mix of gothic and streetwear clothing, largely originating in the 1990s and often associated with bands such as Nirvana.

Light academia: A feminine and airy take on traditional academic, British, Oxford/Cambridge inspired outfits and imagery. For example: floral dresses, lace blouses, chunky cardigans and velvet bows.

Mermaid-core: This aesthetic is inspired by feminine beach looks and imagery of mermaid lore, such as fishing nets, shells and shimmery texts.

Minimalist: An aesthetic that is often applied to both fashion and interiors, meaning neutral, simple and uncluttered styling.

Nautical: A way of dressing that is inspired by what you might typically wear on a boat, including Breton stripes, blue and white colours, loafers and white jeans.

Old Hollywood: An aesthetic defined by the clothing worn by female actresses largely in the 1950s (although the term spans 1920s–1970s), notably Audrey Hepburn and Marilyn Monroe.

Old money: This aesthetic takes inspiration from the stereotypical imagery of an old-money (usually American) family who play tennis, have brunch at the golf club and all went to Yale. Old-money outfits include white tennis skirts, bouclé jackets and little black dresses.

Preppy: The preppy aesthetic is a mix of sporty, feminine and academic styles. These styles are largely inspired by clothes worn by the typical Ivy League student.

Princess-core: A hyper-feminine aesthetic that pulls from fantasy or historical princess silhouettes, featuring miniature bows, round necklines, puff sleeves and ruffles.

Punk: Originating in the '70s and '80s, the punk aesthetic pulls from the British rock scene and is often associated with the work of Vivienne Westwood, including plaid patterns, leather, striped socks and mohawks.

Scandi girl: This aesthetic pulls from minimal and effortless styles typically worn by women in Copenhagen and often inspired by Mathilda Djerf.

Street style: A sporty, avant-garde style of dress inspired by outfits worn at fashion week hubs across the world.

Acknowledgements

This book would not exist without Nicole Thomas, who saw potential in me and gave me the confidence to put my pen to paper. I am so grateful to Nicole and the team at Quercus for putting their trust in my creative instincts, allowing me to change my mind and having faith in me to decide what content belonged in this book. As a literature graduate, it's always been a dream of mine to write a book, but I never imagined I would be so lucky to be given the opportunity to publish.

Thank you to Harriet Webster, who has been an absolute joy to work with as my editor. She reassured me through my doubts, and was always excited about my work when I needed it most.

Thank you to Mietta Yans who created the incredible design of this book; she has brought my words to life in such a beautiful way.

Thank you to my mum, who is my biggest style inspiration. There's so much to say that everything I write feels inadequate. You have always supported me in my dreams with complete faith that I can do whatever I put my mind to.

You have always been the first person I've wanted to show my work to – hopefully this book is a bit better than the drawings I showed you when I was five ... or twenty! Thank you for taking on the brunt of the work for the business while I wrote this book. I would fall apart without you.

Thank you to my dad, who has quietly kept my life running while I try to focus. My dad is the hardest worker I know, and I attribute any success I have had so far to the life he built for us.

Thank you to my boyfriend Arthur, who is always excited about my mad schemes and lets me run on at him for hours. You are the comfort at the end of every day.

To my audience, thank you for your support and interest in my ideas. I would not have had this opportunity without your curiosity, your enthusiasm and your faith in me. We have created such an exciting community full of incredible women: from mothers, to lawyers, to artists. You are all so special and I see the beauty in each of you.

About the author

Ellie-Jean Royden is a personal style consultant, content creator and founder of popular online blog, Body & Style which has amassed a community of over one million across socials. Ellie works with women to help them express their true selves through their clothing, sharing practical styling advice and offering one-to-one consultations and she has been featured in multiple publications including *The New York Times*, *the Express* and *The Sun*. She currently lives in Norfolk in the UK.

First published in Great Britain in 2024
by Greenfinch
An imprint of Quercus Editions Ltd
Carmelite House
50 Victoria Embankment
London
EC4Y 0DZ

An Hachette UK company

Select images on pages 2–21, 24–26, 29, 30–35, 36–39, 41, 42–44, 47, 48, 53, 54, 56, 59, 60, 62, 65, 66, 68, 71–103, 131–132, 143, 145, 147, 149, 151, 153, 155, 157, 159, 161, 163, 165, 165–214, 215 © **Unsplash 2024** / Select images on pages 24, 29, 30, 36, 41, 42, 47, 48, 50, 53, 54, 59, 60, 65, 66, 71, 143, 145, 147, 151, 153, 155, 157, 159, 161, 163, 165 © **Shutterstock 2024** / Select images on pages 24, 217, 219 © **Alamy 2024** / Select images on page 217 © **Getty 2024** / Select images on pages 110–124, 215 © **Marks and Spencer 2024** / Select images on pages 110–124 © **John Lewis PLC 2024**

A CIP catalogue record for this book is available from the British Library.

HB ISBN 978-1-52943-662-4
eBook ISBN 978-1-52943-663-1

Commissioning Editor: Nicole Thomas
Project Editor: Harriet Webster
Copy Editor: Harriet Webster
Picture Research: Harriet Webster
Designer and Illustrator: Mietta Yans

Printed and bound in Germany by Mohn Media

10 9 8 7 6 5 4 3 2 1

MIX
Paper | Supporting
responsible forestry
FSC® C011124

Papers used by Greenfinch are from well-managed forests and other responsible sources.

Many thanks to **Marks and Spencer** and **John Lewis** who kindly provided images for the book.